How To Play Nearly
Everything

by Dallas Cline

The classic introduction to ten folk instruments anyone can play, including kazoo, washboard, spoons, and washtub bass. Experts tell how-to-play, where-to-find and how-to-make. Includes tunes, illustrative photos and diagrams and much more.

Oak Publications
New York/London/Sydney

Acknowledgement

Thanks to Debbie Avidan and Jason Shulman who are a joy of work with, as well as all the wonderful people who contributed to this book... and a special thanks to my daughter, Marnie, for all the time she gave me for so long!

Cover photography by David Gahr

Every reasonable attempt has been made to obtain clearance for the photos appearing on pages 41 and 42.

Order No. OK 63420
International Standard Book Number: 0.8256.0199.1
Library of Congress Catalog Card Number: 77-83767

Exclusive Distributors:
Music Sales Corporation
257 Park Avenue South, New York, NY 10010 USA
Music Sales Limited
8/9 Frith Street, London W1V 5TZ England
Music Sales Pty. Limited
120 Rothschild Street, Rosebery, Sydney, NSW 2018, Australia

Printed in the United States of America by
Vicks Lithograph and Printing Corporation

CONTENTS

INTRODUCTION

There are quite a number of somewhat unusual instruments that have no music written for them specifically, but which have become with time very much a part of our musical tradition. They are certainly worthy of recognition, and the beautiful sounds which many of them produce are a worthwhile addition to our music. It is exciting to learn how to make and play these instruments, because we can incorporate them into our own songs and arrangements of the music we make, or we can take part in all the music being made around us. From the serious group of musicians to the participants at a friendly living room get-together, anyone can include such marvelous instruments as the washtub bass or musical saw in the music-making. These instruments will add that special note one needs for a different sound. Most of them can be learned quickly enough to set up a whole band in a few evenings. A little homework and the next get-together will be sensational!

This book is like having one glorious folk-music festival filled with workshops of all kinds, given by some of the most informed people from all over the country. They bring you the history of many instruments, stories about them, information on making many of them, and explicit details on how to play each one. Some of these musicians even supply music or a tablature to help you in your playing.

These old-timey instruments are just the thing for those people who want to participate in making music but never seem to find the time to study seriously. They DO take time and concentration to play, but can be mastered to some degree in a short period. On the other hand it is usually a big help to have some direction or instruction. You may watch a jug player on TV and think it looks like simple fun—but when you try it, something just isn't right. There are tricks to learn and people to learn them from, and with a little practice you will be a fine addition to any group. You might want to learn how to play the spoons. A teach-in with prize-winning spoons player Barbara Mendelsohn from California will start you off on becoming a popular guest at any party, and she can take you right up to an advanced workshop so you can graduate from the party to the neighborhood band. Or maybe after the teach-in on a nose flute, you will be inspired to write a special "Song for the Nose Flute."

Some of the most interesting groups we've seen on stage have been those with a couple of unorthadox or unusual instruments used for rhythm or melody. Perhaps people perk up and take notice because in their heads they are thinking, "That's something *I* could play!" But there is also the idea of its being novel and different. Some of these instruments alone make a very beautiful accompaniment to certain types of songs, and a performer may want to use them for a change of pace. Unforgettable are some of the washboard solos on the old jug band records by Washboard Sam, and one will always remember hearing Debbie McClatchy singing "Dicey Riley" with nothing but spoons for rhythm. It's the song you always ask her to do again.

Making music is one of the most beautiful things people can do together. It's a very exciting thought to wonder at all the potential musicians out there who will find their way to sharing music because of the people who brought this book together to help them learn how. It may even give this old world a new sound!

Dallas Cline

SUE E. BARBER AND PERCY O. DANFORTH

Sue Barber was born in Iowa and has lived in all parts of the country, staying long enough in Denver to earn a degree in languages and teach there for four years. But her first love has always been music, and she went on to complete a master's degree in ethno-musicology at the University of Michigan. Besides her great interest in the bones, she is a violist and enjoys symphonic and chamber music. She has also studied Chinese music and culture, as well as American folk music. Her current research project and thesis is an in-depth study of the Philadelphia Orchestra's exchange trip to the People's Republic of China in 1973. Sue's other interests include sewing, knitting, reading, travel and art.

Percy Danforth learned to play the bones in Washington, D.C. in 1908. In those days bones playing was more common than it is now. He and his friends gathered in front of Isaac Clayman's grocery store on summer evenings

under the soft light of the gas streetlamps. Young black men from a nearby part of town drifted to the same corner. (There were no streetlights in their section of town.) They danced and accompanied themselves with the bones. These masters of the art were Percy's teachers. After this early instruction, Percy set the bones aside and played them only at odd moments and often with odd equipment, like two rulers. He pursued careers as student, architect, teacher and engineer at various times and in various places. He currently works full-time for Balance Technology in Ann Arbor, Michigan, as personnel director and general doer-of-all-things.

He began concentrating on his bones playing in 1973 when his wife of fifty years bragged about his abilities and urged that he do a public demonstration. From there on the bones took on a life of their own. He has been playing for folk festivals, schools and church groups and making video tapes, tracking down other bones players, and devoting himself to a serious study of how to teach others the art of bones playing.

HOW TO MAKE AND PLAY THE BONES
By Sue E. Barber in collaboration
with Percy O. Danforth

What folk instrument is eminently portable (fits in a pocket), inexpensive to buy or make (from various scrap materials), easy to play (compared to many other instruments), entertaining to hear and watch (evoking laughter and hand-clapping), prehistoric in origin but still played (especially at folk and ragtime festivals), and relatively little known? One last hint. The generic name identifies the scraps from which the original models were made. Ah, yes. . . . This must be "the bones."

Despite their many appearances at various places and times during man's sojourn through history, the bones have not been widely known or played in the past fifty years or so. Fortunately, the recent renewal of interest in folk music and ethnic cultures has generated something of a bones revival as well. We invite you, in these next few pages, to participate in this revival. Your role is a pleasant one. First read the historical section of this chapter so that you can fully appreciate the antiquity of your recently-discovered interest. Then get yourself a pair of bones and carefully follow our instructions for playing them. Within a few weeks, you too should be on your way to becoming part of an informal fraternity of bones players that stretches back into the mists of pre-history.

History

Bones are a percussion instrument. They are defined in scholarly terms as idiophones. ". . . the substance of the instrument itself, owing to its solidarity and elasticity, yields the sounds. . . . Concussion idiophones or clappers are two or more complimentary sonorous parts struck against each-other." (Von Hornbostel and Sachs 1961: 14) The two "complimentary sonorous parts" were originally, indeed, two pieces of bone. Later, various types of wood were used to make bones. Whatever material they are made of, such instruments are extensions of clapping hands and stamping feet.

Bones are always played in the plural. They consist of two parts, held between the fingers of the hand. They strike together as the player manipulates his wrist and arm to produce various rhythms. The bones shown in the photographs are 7 3/8 inches long, 1 inch wide, and 5/16 to 3/8 inches thick. The length and thickness may vary slightly with the material of which particular bones are made. The pieces are usually slightly curved, allowing greater ease in holding them and greater flexibility of movement.

Research reveals that the bones in some form date back almost as far as man himself. The specific origins of the instrument are unknown, but they are probably among the earliest musical instruments made by man. Bones have been found in graves excavated in Moldavia (in southeastern Europe), dating from the Second Millennium, B.C. Mosaics found in the ruins of the ancient city of Ur in Mesopotamia show the bones. Egyptian vases dating from 3000 B.C. depict female dancers playing bones. In ancient Greece, bones were associated with the worship of the goddess Hathor, goddess of heaven, joy and death.

During the Middle Ages jongleurs wandered throughout Europe singing, dancing and playing various instruments, including the bones. Book illustrations and miniatures from the 9th century onward show the bones in combination with various other contemporary instruments. In addition to their musical functions during these centuries, the bones were also used as signals by lepers, who sounded them to warn others of their approach (Marcuse 1964: 105).

By the 12th century, bones seem to have centered themselves in northwestern Europe. A reference from the *Book of Leinster* (ca. 1160) summarized the prevailing attitude of the Irish toward bones players.

Pipes, fiddle, men of no valour, bone-players and pipe players, a crowd hideous, noisy, profane, shriekers and shouters.

(quoted in McCoullough 1976)

Three centuries later Shakespeare mentioned bones in *A Midsummer Night's Dream.* Inigo Jones used them in his 17th century court masques. (A masque was a lavish stage production that combined poetry, music, dancing and acting.) Bones are still played in the pubs of northern England and Ireland in ensembles to accompany dancing. They also remain a popular children's toy in both Britain and Holland.

In the United States, bones playing has been associated most commonly with slavery and minstrelsy. Some writers have conjectured that bones came to the States from Africa and were part of African musical traditions which were continued in the slave quarters of America. Available evidence documents the existence of the bones primarily in South Africa, however, and black South African bones players have admitted that they derived the idea from European missionaries (Kirby 1934: 10). This information, coupled with the fact that most slaves were abducted from West Africa, not from the southern part of the continent, makes an African origin of the instrument unlikely. More feasible is the notion that the bones came to the New World with immigrants from Northern Europe. Slaves saw the bones being played by these white settlers. Because the materials were readily available and the techniques of playing were easily learned, the blacks appropriated the bones. In the process of adaption, the slaves added layers of rhythmic syncopation that were remnants from their African musical traditions. Letters and other accounts during the 18th and 19th centuries describe slave bands on plantations and roving street bands, the latter sometimes made up of freemen, tootling for pennies on street corners. Both groups used bones as part of the ensemble.

The first blackface minstrel show was presented in 1843 in New York City. The four original blackface performers combined singing, dancing and joking into a fast-paced variety show format that was an instant success. Their instruments were fiddle, tambourine, banjo and bones; a combination similar to that often used in itinerant black bands. One of the standard characters in the show was Brudder Bones. He was a comic as well as a musician. For the entertainment of his audiences, he tossed his bones in the air, juggled them, even stood on his head while playing. He could imitate drums, marches, reveille, and horse races with his bones. In his more musically-oriented moments, he used his bones to provide a steady beat for the singing and dancing. He could also create intricate rhythm patterns that elaborated the overall complexity of the musical texture.

As the minstrel show evolved into an extravaganza later in the 19th century, the bones were shunted aside in favor of other instruments. But they continued to be played on street corners, in markets, schoolyards, parlors and in dance halls, by both black and white musicians. Many of today's players, including Percy Danforth, are elderly men who learned the art of bones playing many years ago from the performers whose roots go back to the showmen of minstrelsy days.

Where To Find or How To Make Your Own Bones

Before you can begin to play the bones, you must have a pair to work with. Actually, you need two pairs. The American school of bones playing requires that the performer stand while playing and use a pair of bones in each hand. British bones players on the contrary, generally play while sitting down and use bones in only one hand.

Bones are available commercially from some music stores and by catalog order. They are frequently on sale at folk festivals, especially if you are fortunate enough to encounter Master Bones Artist Percy Danforth.

You can also make your own bones. Simply cut slabs of anything you want, to the dimensions described in the diagram.

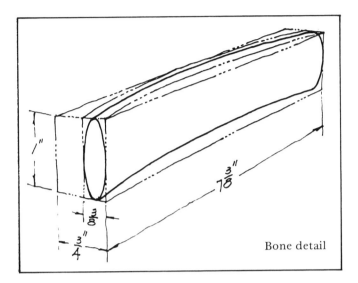

Bone detail

Different materials will yield different sound colors. Hardwoods such as rosewood, birch or ebony have a piercing, shrill quality. Softer materials, pine or walnut, are softer in tone. Or you may want to make the real thing . . . bone bones. In that case, cut the rib bones of sheep or cattle to the desired length. Rib bones are best because they have the proper natural curvature. Scrape the bones clean and allow them to bleach and dry in the sun. Sand and polish them with emery cloth until they are smooth.

Some Helpful Hints on Bones Playing

One often hears the phrase "rattle the bones" used as a description of bones playing. Actually that characterization is a misnomer. Good bones playing is far more than a noise and clatter produced at random by waving the hands and arms around in the air with pieces of wood or bone stuck between the fingers. There are certain basic movements that you must master carefully before you can begin to combine them into more interesting forms. Your eventual goal as a bones player is to be able to do more than merely reinforce the beat of a piece of accomanying music. You want to be able to enhance the texture of that music with your playing by elaborating a continuous series of rhythmic patterns. This sophisticated patterning that is the mark of the true bones virtuoso requires precision, discipline and practice. Remember, the bones are, above all, a musical instrument, and they must be used with respect and played with understanding and skill.

As you begin to play the bones, there are several things to keep in mind in order to produce successful results:

1. Practice is a must. The practice sessions needn't be long, and they should be enjoyable, but you do need to keep at it on a regular basis.

2. American style bones playing requires a high degree of ambidexterity. Most people are more facile with one hand than the other. Nevertheless, start using bones in both hands from the outset. Otherwise the tendency is to allow your less facile hand to lag behind in its development, and that will slow down your progress in general. It will probably take more time to build up real control with your "other" hand. But the real secret of great bones playing is the ability to produce different rhythms with each hand at the same time. It takes time and practice to develop this high level of coordination, but keep working towards that goal.

3. Thoroughly learn the rudiments we describe in the following pages. Try combining them in as many ways as you can. Don't just string the rudiments together time after time. Variation of order, accent and dynamic level are all important. Be creative. Experiment.

4. Most important of all is to STAY LOOSE. RELAX your whole body as you play. The bones are really an extension of the body itself. The virtuoso player does not merely play; he dances the bones. Get your whole body moving and play from the soles of your feet to the tip of your cowlick.

5. While the previous statements concerning the dedication and discipline required to master the bones are all true, playing them should be FUN. In spite of its long history, this is not a stately, prissy instrument. Its masters and carriers of the tradition have usually been the folk, not the mannered gentry. Play the bones in the spirit of festivity and celebration that surrounded medieval feast days, pub dancing, village weddings and minstrel shows.

Holding the Bones

When observing a virtuoso in action, you will see only a plethora of rapid movement and hear a lot of intricate patterning. But don't let all the sound and fury intimidate you. Those rhythms are built upon the few basic movements or rudiments which follow. As you work, study the accompanying photographs carefully and imitate them precisely for best results.

First, you must know how to hold the bones properly. (Actually there are variations in the ways bones are held, but the method described here has proved to be the easiest for beginners to master.) In performance the bones move so rapidly that it is impossible to see that only one bone moves. The moving bone is held between the third and fourth fingers with the end extending about ¼ inch above the knuckles. Pull the ring finger back, place it on the edge of the bone, and press the bone firmly into the pad between the ring and middle fingers.

Position of the moveable bone:

The bone must *never* touch the palm of the hand. If it does, you will not get any sound because the bone cannot move. Press your little finger against your ring finger to help hold the bone in place. This bone is a spring; you must maintain the tension on it at all times.

The other bone is held stationary between the second and third fingers of the hand. It should extend above the knuckles ½ inch higher than the moveable bone. Jam the stationary bone against the heel of the hand and cup the hand around it. Press the thumb against the first finger to help hold this bone in place.

Position of the stationary bone:

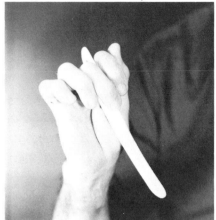

When both bones are in the proper position, the tips are not quite parallel horizontally. The tips should be ⅛ to ¹⁄₁₆ of an inch apart. The convex sides of the bones face inward.

Both bones in proper playing position:

When appropriate movements of the wrist and arm are made, the spring-like tension maintained on the moveable bone allows it to move slightly, striking the anvil bone, and thus producing sound.

Contrary to what you might expect, the bones are not played by moving the fingers. The fingers in fact, must not move at all. Their function is simply to keep the pieces of the instrument in proper alignment. Movements of the wrist, arm and shoulder actually produce the sounds. When you play, extend your arms away from your body; keep your elbows bent. At first your arms will tire easily, but as you continue practicing, you will build up your muscle tone for longer and longer playing sessions. Remember to RELAX. That will improve your playing and lessen the fatigue at the same time.

Playing the Bones

The Tap (The Single Tap)

The simplest form of rhythm is a single tap. Align the bones properly in your hand and extend your arms. Tilt your hand toward the center of your body as shown in the photo.

Before snap of hand:

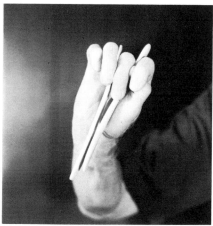

After snap of hand:

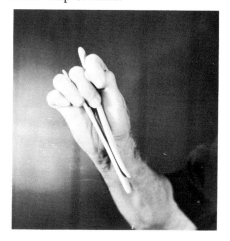

Snap your hand outward from the wrist, a quick, sharp movement. At the same time your forearm will move slightly toward your body. You should hear a tap as the moving bone strikes the anvil. If your tap doesn't happen, check for the following: Are the bones too far apart? Are they touching? Are you allowing the bones to move? (If so, the tips will miss each other when you move your arm to tap.)

Practice the tap many times, slowly, with each hand, until you have mastered the feel of the movement. Then try alternating taps with both hands.

As soon as you master even one or two movements, you will want to begin working with musical accompaniment. Playing the bones without music is like trying to dance without music. . . . It just isn't very satisfying. Many types of music make good background for bones playing. The bones accommodate most readily to music with a 2/4 or 4/4 meter. Percy works most often with ragtime. Minstrel show tunes, marches, jazz, pop tunes and string band music are possibilities. Jigs, reels, waltzes and Spanish numbers present different kinds of rhythmic challenges. Start with songs that are relatively simple rhythmically, and graduate to more complex pieces as your skill develops. At the same time, begin with simple movements,

single taps and rolls, and work up fancier routines as you feel able to create them. You don't have to know how to read music to play the bones, but you must always be sensitive to the underlying meter or pulse of a particular song. Feel this beat and elaborate on it in your playing. Different meters require varied types of bones patterns, however. The chart below should help to illustrate the differences between a march rhythm and a jig rhythm, for example. Sing the basic beat to yourself and then try tapping the bones to each beat. You will sense immediately that the feel of the two meters is not the same and that you must adjust your playing accordingly.

Building Your Skill

The Double Tap (The Flam)

There are several ways of producing a double tap. The easiest is to combine two single taps,

one executed with each hand, one right after the other. In other words, tap once with each hand, compressing the temporal space between the two, to an instant. An alternate method of double tapping is to reverse the motion of the single tap. Instead of snapping your hand outward, snap it toward the center of your body. In addition to the single tap, the recoil as your hand returns to its neutral position will produce a second tap or backlash.

The Extended Roll

The roll or trill sounds like a continuous series of very rapid taps. The arm movement is the crucial element. Hold your bones so that their tips are halfway between your elbow and the tops of the bones. Keep the tips in that same position and move your hand across the front of your body *at the same time* that you move your elbow away from your body. Then do the reverse movement and keep alternating. Actually, the top of the hand describes an arc with the tips of the bones as the center of rotation.

Note: The tips of the bones remain in virtually the same place as the arm and wrist rotate.

To learn the movement, try holding the tips of the bones stationary with your free hand, so there is no sound. Then move your wrist and arm in the prescribed manner. Now release the tips, allowing them to sound. Start slowly and gradually increase the speed of the wrist-arm rotation. The whole thing is a whip-like motion originating in the shoulder and travelling down through the arm through the tips of the bones. Be careful as you build up speed. The tendency is to want to suspend movement along the shoulder-arm-wrist axis and degenerate into rotation of the lower arm. Watching yourself in a mirror will be helpful as you master this movement. Keep your eye on your wrist and elbow, and be sure they are always moving in opposite directions. Listen carefully to the sound you produce as you build up speed. Just like a violin trill, your bones trill needs to be fast but not muddy-sounding.

The Triplet

The triplet is really a reduced roll. There are three taps on a single beat, just as in notated music. It involves a crosswise motion of the hand in front of the body. Extend the arm to the side of the body and pull it sharply in towards the center of the body. As the arm snaps across the body, the moving bone should spring against the anvil three times, once at the outer edge of the motion, once in the center (really the recoil from the previous tap), and once at the inner edge.

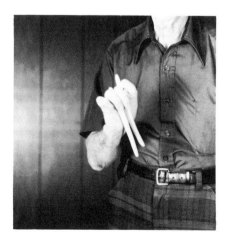

Relative hand position for each of the three taps of the movement.

The movement resembles an "S" on its side, as the picture indicates.

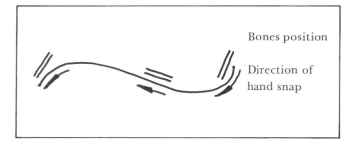

Bones position

Direction of hand snap

The Four-Beat Roll (The Four-Beat Ruff)

Here you combine a triplet with a final tap. Use the same movement as for the triplet above, but complete the "S" to form an "8." Add a final tap as you complete the sweep of the arm.

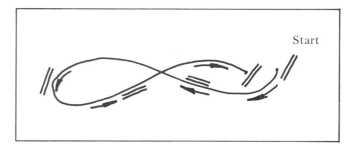

Start

The Crescendo

It is possible to produce a crescendo by controlling and manipulating the relative positions of the two bones. To begin softly, the bones are held so that they strike high up, near the fingers of the hand. As the crescendo builds, gradually change the position of the moveable bone, so that it strikes the anvil lower and lower down.

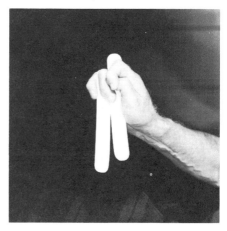
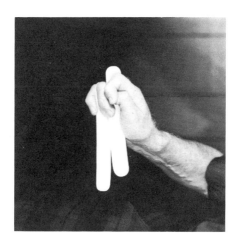
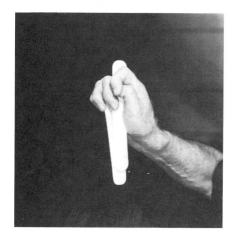

Relative position of the two bones, pianissimo to fortissimo.

The crescendo reaches full volume when the bones are aligned so that their tips are in normal playing position. These adjustments of alignment are also the proper method of varying the dynamic level of your playing.

Accents

Accents are stresses of certain beats. To accent any motion or any point in a roll, snap the hand harder than you would normally. The harder snap will cause the bones to strike with additional force on that beat (or off-beat), thus making it stand out from those around it. You will normally want to strike the strong beats of a piece with a little more force in order to reinforce the underlying rhythm.

Accents are also essential to the development of syncopated rhythmic patterns. A syncopation is the deliberate displacement of the normal pulse of a piece of music. To syncopate, you may shift the accent from a strong beat to a weak beat, or you may divide a beat into several smaller parts, perhaps holding one of them over to the next beat. Accent your syncopations to make them more audible. They add interest to the progression of the tune and the texture of the music.

Making Music

It is impossible to describe in this short chapter every syncopated rhythmic pattern a bones virtuoso can produce. All rhythms are variations of the single, double and triple taps, and the roll. By altering the regularity of the taps or by extending or delaying them, you can rearrange the order of sonic events into complex rhythmic patterns. The possible combinations are virtually endless. As we mentioned before, you will want to create patterns that elaborate on the meter, not merely reinforce it. These elaborations are the element that makes bones playing fun to do and enjoyable to hear and watch.

As you gain dexterity, you will want to begin using cross rhythms. This involves starting a pattern in one hand, picking it up with the other, and perhaps tossing it back to the first. You will also want to try executing different patterns simultaneously in each hand. Work up your coordination gradually and increase the complexity and ambidexterity of your patterning as your skill evolves.

Due to the mingling of a number of influences particular to America with earlier bones playing technique, a unique style has emerged here. American-style playing is flamboyant, elaborate, and complex in use of rhythmic patterns and syncopated elements. As it has emerged in the American milieu, bones playing is a stand-up art form. This is performance bones; the player is really a soloist and a center of attention in the best sense of the word. He is an entertainer, a dancer, and a musician who merges his being and his instrument into one unit as he plays

As any entertainer knows, the smell of the crowd is a significant element of his dedication and his willingness to spend hours practicing and perfecting his art. As a bones player in the American tradition of entertainment, you too, will want to seek out fellow performers and an audience. As soon as you begin to perfect your skills, locate performers on other instruments (piano, fiddle, guitar or banjo, for example) and begin making live music together. You will find that kind of playing much more rewarding than performing at home for your cat. You and your fellow musicians will soon want to graduate to performing for an audience, even if it's only a gathering of family and friends. You will quickly find that the bones are a real show-stealer. Your audience will be amazed that you can produce so many intricate rhythms with four little sticks. Many of them will have never heard bones before, so you and your playing will be a delightful surprise.

Now you have the basic instruction you need to begin to develop your own expertise as a bones virtuoso. So get busy. Practice. Play. Create. And above all, enjoy yourself and your new art.

Bibliography

Blades, James. *Percussion Instruments and Their History.* New York: Frederick A. Praeger, 1970.

Buchner, Alexander. *Musical Instruments Through the Ages.* London: Batchworth Press Limited, 1961.

George, Zelma Watson. *A Guide to Negro Music.* PhD. thesis for New York University, 1953.

Hughes, Langston and Meltzer, Milton. *Black Magic.* Englewood Cliffs, New Jersey: Prentice Hall, 1967.

Marcuse, Sybil. *Musical Instruments: A Comprehensive Dictionary.* Garden City, New York: Doubleday and Co., 1964.

McCoullough, L.E. *The Complete Irish Tinwhistle Tutor*. Pittsburg: Silver Speak Publications, 1976.

Nathan, Hans. *Dan Emmett and the Rise of Early Negro Minstrelsy*. Norman, Oklahoma: University of Oklahoma Press, 1962.

Paskman, Daley and Speath, Sigmund. *Gentlemen, Be Seated!* Garden City, New York: Doubleday, Doran, and Co., 1928.

Rice, Edward Leroy. *Monarchs of Minstrelsy*. New York: Kenny Publishing Co., 1911.

Sachs, Curt. *The History of Musical Instruments*. New York: W.W. Norton, 1940.

Toll, Robert C. *Blacking Up: The Minstrel Show in Nineteenth Century America*. New York: Oxford University Press, 1974.

Von Hornbostel, Eric and Sachs, Curt. "The Classification of Musical Instruments," *Galpin Society Journal*, No. 14, 1961.

Discography

Louis Beaudoin
Philo Records 2000
The Chieftains
(Imported), Five Records, Claddagh Records Ltd. CC2, CC7, CC10, CC14, CC16

MARTY SACHS

Marty Sachs grew up in western Connecticut, surrounded with bluegrass and folk music in a very musical family. He plays a string of instruments including the guitar, fiddle, and mandolin, but the first thing he tried, because it seemed easy, was the jaw harp. He tells us that after he learned to keep his teeth out of the way, it was great fun! He grew up to become a full-time professional musician, and has played with several bands, finding that an occasional jaw harp solo never fails to bring down the house. At the present time he is primarily a bass fiddle player with a Boston bluegrass band, Northern Lights. He does some harp playing on banjoist Roger Sprung's album *Roger and Joan*, and also with Joan Sprung on her second Folk Legacy album, *Pictures to My Mind*.

HOW TO PLAY THE JAW HARP
By Marty Sachs

That happy, twangy sound heard in a string band is a jaw harp. This chapter has to do with learning about that instrument, finding a good one and starting to play it.

The jaw harp appears to be one of the oldest musical instruments, and was referred to as a "jaw's harp" approximately 1595, although instruments like it were seen in Asia about 1350. The first jaw harps were made of wood. Bamboo was used for those found on Formosa and the Philippine Islands. These primitive jaw harps looked like oversized clothes-pins with lamellas or tongues made to vibrate by a series of jerks from a cord.

In the Austrian Alps, around the mid-19th century, jaw harps were played by boys trying to woo their sweethearts. To this day it is still used in Austria for the same purpose.

Purchasing a Good Jaw Harp

Every jaw harp is different so you should try as many as possible before purchasing one. Before you buy, carefully check the metal tongue. If it has any excessive rust, hairline cracks, or if the tongue does not lie perfectly flat on the frame, it would be best to check another instrument. Any harp having any of the listed imperfections is more than likely going to suffer from poor tone, or else will eventually break.

Jaw harps come in many shapes and sizes. There are basically two styles available in North America; the English and American style harps. The English harp will often be the first choice of the novice because of its eye-catching design, and low price. They usually start as low as $1.50. However, for the serious-minded jaw harpist or jaw harpy, this is really not a good bargain. The metal tongue is usually thinner than in the American style harp and results in a softer volume. The English model is also a little more awkward to hold, and generally has a shorter life span than its American counterpart. The most popular brand of English harp is the "Bruce Harp." In a situation where the harp should be heard well, try using the American style harp. I find it to be more comfortable, also. There are several good brands of American jaw harps. The Smith harp, the Rich harp and the Snoopy harp are among the best known. These harps usually start at about $2.50 and may be sold for as high as $5.00. It is well worthwhile getting a good one.

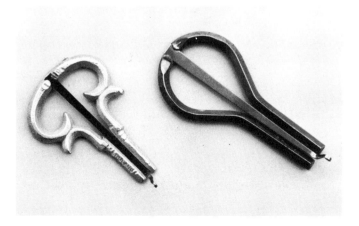

Holding the Jaw Harp

I have found two comfortable ways to hold the harp. One way is to cup your left hand (if you're right-handed). Holding the palm of your left hand toward your mouth, place the jaw harp in the cupped area of your hand in a vertical position, with the narrow part of the metal tongue pointing away from your face.

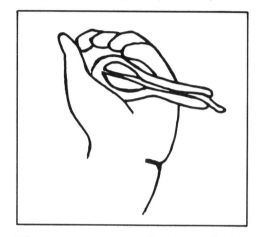

This way is particularly good if you're playing music with louder instruments and you find it necessary to hear yourself. Your hand is actually projecting the sound of the harp back to your ear. The second method is to hold your left hand the opposite way and hold the top of the harp with your index finger and the bottom of the frame with your thumb. I find this way to be more comfortable than the other, and it also helps to project the sound of the jaw harp forward.

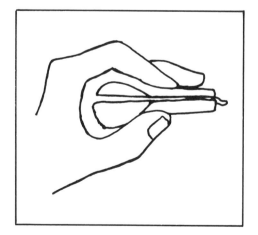

The easiest way to hold the harp in your mouth is to begin by gently pressing the harp against your teeth, with your teeth open just enough to let the tongue of the jaw harp pass through, usually about ¼ of an inch. The most natural way to pluck the metal tongue is to pluck it away from your face with your right hand (opposite if you're left-handed). If you get a buzz, this means either the metal tongue is hitting the frame of the harp because you are squeezing too hard, or the metal tongue is hitting your teeth because your teeth are closed too much. If this happens you should separate your teeth more.

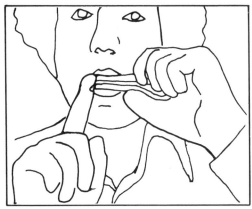

Playing the Jaw Harp

Presuming that you are able to get a clear tone, we will continue. When playing the jaw harp, your mouth acts as a sound cavity, very much the way the body of a guitar acts as a resonating chamber when the strings are strummed. If you make the oral cavity smaller by moving your tongue higher in your mouth, (the same manner in which you would whistle) you will get a higher pitch to emanate from the harp. By moving your tongue down, you will get a deeper pitch. Breath evenly while playing notes through the harp, and then try breathing lightly and heavily to vary the tone. With a little practice you will find that you will actually be able to play tunes note for note. By plucking both ways, you can also vary the rhythm and add twice as many notes.

The best tunes to start with are the simple ones in which the melody is familiar. You can play any simple tune which you can sing or hum. "Choose Your Partner" and "Yankee Doodle" are ideal tunes.

Some Final Hints

When playing with other musicians the jaw harp is used as both a rhythm and solo instrument. Generally it should blend in, standing out only during the jaw harp solo. When not in use it is a good idea to keep the jaw harp in a small bag or box to keep it from becoming rusted or bent.

The jaw harp is an instrument that anyone can play. These pages should help you through the initial stages as you attain basic mastery of the jaw harp. With a little more practice, you can become a veritable virtuoso. So have fun!

SALLY F. CUTLER

Sally Cutler describes herself as a poet living in Syracuse, New York, who makes her living playing the kazoo. Actually, she grew up on Long Island in New York, and has been living upstate for about ten years. Her earliest musical memories involve being lulled to sleep by her father's boogie-woogie piano playing. She went on to study flute, where she learned a lot of useful kazoo techniques, and to sing in many, many choruses and choirs. She discovered her native ability on the kazoo while riding a shuttle bus at college in Albany.

Sally now lives with her husband in Syracuse where she has just completed a Masters degree in creative writing (poetry) and plays the kazoo and autoharp with *Cranberry Lake*, a band playing old-time and jug band music.

HOW TO PLAY THE KAZOO
by Sally F. Cutler

I hand people my kazoo and, because they've not any too recently played a kazoo, they blow into it. They make the mistake of confusing the kazoo with some woodwind, brass or reed instrument. In fact, the kazoo is more an amplifier than an instrument. It amplifies a sound which you make—a hum or some singing. Its sound mechanism vibrates because you *make* it vibrate with your voice. But that is its advantage. Its limits are only those of the player, and with practice, that player can successfully make it imitate a saxophone, trumpet or clarinet.

The kazoo is a tube with a hole cut into its wall. Over the hole is a vibrator. Kazoos may be made from a number of materials. Early ones were carved in wood. The ones most commonly available now are either metal or plastic. The plastic kazoo is pretty much a failure. Its problem seems to be that the whole body vibrates and the sound gets out of control. Metal kazoos (made by The Kazoo Company in Eden, New York, the only producer of metal kazoos in the world) hold up better and, if set up properly, sound best.

According to Maurice Spectoroff of The Kazoo Company, the kazoo may be the only truly American Instrument. It was probably derived from something like a wood flute. Early wooden kazoos had finger holes in them, although these did absolutely nothing to alter the sound. (Kazoos today still have mock finger holes imprinted on them.) The earliest kazoo known of by The Kazoo Company is a 1904 wood example. The standard metal kazoo has been made since 1915.

Setting Up Your Kazoo

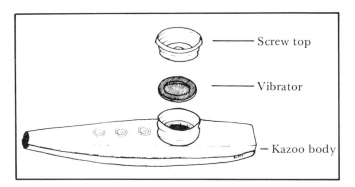

Figure 1 Exploded view of the kazoo. From top to bottom are the screw top, the vibrator (membrane shown with cross-hatching), and the kazoo body.

The kazoo vibrator is the heart of the instrument. What the vibrator is made of and how it is set up determines the quality of the sound. "Wax paper," you say? Well, some of those plastic kazoos use wax paper, and of course, comb players use wax paper. But real kazoo vibrators are made from the stomach linings of lambs. No substitute has been found to have the necessary qualities of strength, resilience and tone. Large sheets of this membrane are pasted over a sheet of cardboard, which is, more accurately, a sheet of holes-in-cardboard. The glue goes on the cardboard and the mem-

brane is placed down over it. The membrane is free of glue where it stretches across the openings. This is not an easy job and lots of times the membrane gets a little fold in it, or a small hole or tear, or it gets some glue on it. Also the membrane isn't always of uniform thickness. The sheet of cardboard is cut in a large cutting machine. Sometimes the sheet isn't exactly square; some finished vibrators are off center. As you can see, lots can go wrong at this point. But a membrane vibrator in no matter what shape (unless it's really ripped in half) is better than any piece of wax paper.

When you go to buy a kazoo, try to get one with a smooth, tight, flawless vibrator. It is easy enough to unscrew the top of the kazoo and look in at the vibrator. You can take it right out; it's not attached to anything.

Setting up the vibrator is the first trick all prospective kazoo virtuosos should learn. The sound dynamics of the instrument are such that the player wants to achieve the ideal balance between kazoo "razz" and tone control. So, take your kazoo and unscrew the top. Nine times out of ten, the vibrator is in there with the membrane on the bottom and the cardboard ring on top. Turn it over. This simple action increases the tonal range of the kazoo about one hundred percent, by enabling you to put a wider range of pressure directly on the membrane. Now, screw the top back on just a little. Hum "Melancholy Baby" (or some other appropriate tune) into the kazoo. It probably sounds really razzy. Now screw the top down as tightly as you can. You'll find that the kazoo either makes no sound at all, or that a great deal of the razz has been eliminated. As you gradually unscrew the top, you'll hear the razz come back. You should set the kazoo up for the sound you want. A loose vibrator is great for kazoo marching bands; if you want to play jazz, you'll want it a good deal tighter.

Differences in Kazoos

There are lots of variations on kazoo bodies. Perhaps you have seen the trombone-kazoo or something like it. Most of these are sight gags. The trombone-kazoo, for example, has a moveable slide which doesn't really do anything since it alters the length of the kazoo body, and that, of course, has nothing to do with sound production in the kazoo. The only body variation I have seen that does have different sound properties is the Concert or Hi-Fi Kazoo. The reason for its being louder is that the opening in the screw top over the vibrator is the same size as the opening in the kazoo body, and the same size as the membrane part of the vibrator. This enables the kazoo to function at maximum loudness capacity. The horn on the Concert Kazoo helps too, by directing the sound and so amplifying it somewhat. The Concert Kazoo lends itself to being effectively muted by a partial blockage of the horn. The best mute I've found is a 1¼ inch drain stopper.

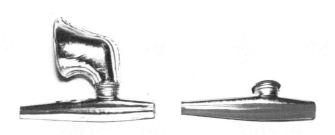

Figure 2 The Concert or Hi-Fi Kazoo (left) and the standard kazoo. Both have metal bodies.

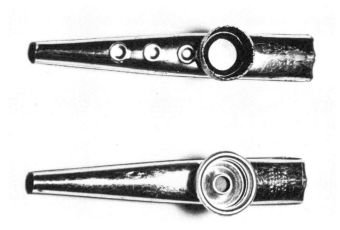

Figure 3 The Concert or Hi-Fi Kazoo (top) with the horn removed, and the standard kazoo. Both kazoos have their screw tops attached; note the difference in diameter of the opening in the screw tops of the Concert and the standard kazoos.

Playing the Kazoo

Once you have your kazoo set up properly, the thing to work on is your technique. While it is true that almost anyone can play the kazoo, to play it well you must at least be able to carry a tune. And while it is also true that most people hum into a kazoo, to really get the most out of it, you will have to perfect a kind of highly controlled singing.

When I play, I make a sound somewhat like a strangulated falsetto; it comes from the very top of my lungs. It is not forced, because it need not be very loud in and of itself to sound loud through the kazoo. This kind of top-of-the-voice sound is relatively easy to control. It is flexible, easy to stop and start, and moves around readily. If you set out to imitate a horn playing be-bop in an upper range, you won't be far wrong. Experiment. Push all kinds of sound through the kazoo and see what happens.

To increase your control and phrasing, you should work on tonguing. If you have ever played a wind instrument, you know what I mean. Place your tongue just behind and above your upper front teeth and say "teh." This lets you make a sudden plosive sound. You can fit it into your kazoo singing to shape your phrases.

You can also "wail" through a kazoo. Make a phony forced vibrato in your throat (like you were imitating a bad opera singer). This is not always easy to control and should be used sparingly. "Flutter tonguing" is also best reserved as a special effect. Place your tongue much as you would for tonguing and then push air past it making it flutter. It's the noise kids make to imitate motor-boats and such.

A "wah-wah" sound presents some interesting problems. To make a "wah-wah" (or "mama doll") sound, you have to stretch your mouth open. Now, how can you keep your mouth around the kazoo and do this? I hold my kazoo in my left hand, making a small circle or OK sign with my thumb and first finger. I put my lips on the back of these fingers and hold the kazoo with the other fingers of that hand so that my first finger and thumb make a seal between the end of the kazoo and my mouth. Now if I stretch my mouth around while I'm singing, I have some flexibility. I've also found that I can get a very high degree of control by closing my fingers down, thus forcing the sound through an even smaller tube than the kazoo itself.

Finally, with the kazoo held as I've already described, you can get a variation on tonguing which I call "lipping." Rather than sounding a "t", you form a "b" sound with your lips. I've never seen a wind instrument player do that!

What comes after you master all this technique is practice and a lot of listening. Lots of old and not-so-old Jug Bands use kazoos (*Cannon's Jug Stompers, The Memphis Jug Band,* and *Jim Kweskin and the Jug Band* among them), but these bands tend to play up the kazoo razz and play down tone. Listen instead to the fiddles, horns and clarinets in the old Jug Bands. And listen to lots of other jazz. The kazoo can be played to imitate the phrasing of a clarinet line. At the same time, it can be tonally controlled so as to imitate a cornet or trumpet. With a little more sound in your throat and some work on high squawks, you can get a decent tenor saxophone. But only a feeling for jazz will enable you to make the kazoo really work.

Of course, jazz is not the only place for kazoos. Classical music is not beyond your grasp and the marching kazoo band may yet become a national institution. Moreover, kazoos are being used to help deaf children vocalize and to encourage senior citizens to strut their stuff. And, I suppose, it's only a matter of time before someone electrifies the kazoo and we all become amplifier-toting superstars.

BEEDLE -UM -BUM
Arranged for Kazoo by Sally Cutler

I play this Kazoo introduction much as it appears on the album, *Jim Kweskin and the Jug Band* (Vanguard), where the kazoo is played by Bruno Wolf. The technique is aimed at making the most of the syncopations. It is actually played in $\frac{2}{4}$ time, but I have put it into $\frac{4}{4}$ because it will be easier for you to count out. Here's the code you will need to read the tablature:

L: Lip
T: Tongue
WA: Wah
WL: Wail
TWA: Accentuate the Wah with a Tongue.
P: Pow — hit the note with a Lip and then drop the pitch and volume slightly, as though you were saying "Pow!"

BEEDLE-UM-BUM

Arranged for kazoo, Sally F. Cutler

Selected and Annotated Discography

This is a selective list of jug band recordings featuring kazoos. It was, of course, in the jug bands that the kazoo was treated as a significant musical instrument.

The list is set up so that the name of the band appears first, followed by a list of tunes they've recorded which feature kazoo. For each tune the date and place of recording are given, followed by the LP on which the cut appears. Finally, for some tunes there are notations about the kazoo player and his style.

Cannon's Jug Stompers
"Mule Get Up in the Alley," October 3, 1929, Memphis, Tennessee. *The Jug Bands* (RF Records, 6).
The kazoo player is Hosea Woods.
Dallas Jamboree Jug Band
"Elm Street Woman Blues," September 20, 1935, Dallas, Texas. *The Jug, Jook and Washboard Bands* (Blues Classic, 2).
The kazoo is probably played by Carl Davis who does a straightforward blues–style break in a tone imitative of a clarinet or fiddle.
The Five Harmaniacs

"Coney Island Washboard," September 17, 1926, place unknown. *Jugs, Washboards and Kazoos* (RCA Victor Vintage Series, LPV–540).
"It Takes a Good Woman," probably September 17, 1926, place unknown. *Jugs, Washboards and Kazoos* (RCA Victor Vintage Series, LPV–540).
"Sadie Green Vamp of New Orleans," September 17, 1926, place unknown. *Jugs, Washboards and Kazoos* (RCA Victor Vintage Series, LPV–540). There is a second kazoo here; the player is unknown.
"What Makes My Baby Cry?" February 8, 1927, place unknown. *Jugs, Washboards and Kazoos* (RCA Victor Vintage Series, LPV–540). Clyde Shugart, who plays kazoo here, has a very mouthy style. He does some tonguing.
Ed Kelly's Washboard Band
"Shim Shaming," August 5, 1937, Charlotte, North Carolina. *The Jug, Jook and Washboard Bands* (Blues Classics, 2).
This tune is essentially "Mama Don't 'Low". The kazoo player is unknown. The band has a novel quality throughout; the kazoo is extremely razzy and the player improvises a little.

Jim Kweskin and the Jug Band
Jim Kweskin and the Jug Band (Vanguard, VSD–2158).
Jug Band Music (Vanguard, VRS–9163).
Relax Your Mind (Vanguard, VSD–79188).
See Reverse Side for Title Vanguard, (VSD-79234).
Garden of Joy (Reprise, 6266).
These people formed what is certainly the most well-known of the 1960s revival bands and are a whole story in themselves. The kazoo assignments were variable; Geoff Muldaur did much of the kazoo work, but Bruno Wolf and Maria D'Amato Muldaur also played. Some of the kazoo playing is mouthy, some has a razzy tone. Sometimes it is difficult to tell if one is hearing the kazoo or Kweskin's comb playing. The band appears (with somewhat changeable personnel), on the records listed here.
The Memphis Jug Band
"Newport News Blues," February 24, 1927, place unknown. *Jugs, Washboards and Kazoos* (RCA Victor Vintage Series, LVP–540).
Ben Ramey, who plays on these cuts, is certainly the most accomplished kazoo player to have been recorded during the Jug Band era. He has a fine sense of jazz lines and fills, treats the kazoo as a legitimate instrument (often working in counterpoint with the harmonica), and demonstrates a use of such techniques as tonguing and flutter-tonguing. Note especially Ramey's excellent blues work.
"Sun(sic.) Brimmers Blues," February 24, 1927, place unknown. *Jugs, Washboards and Kazoos* (RCA Victor Vintage Series, LPV–540). Son Brimmer was Will Shade's (the leader of the Memphis Jug Band) nickname.
"Coal Oil Blues," February 13, 1928, Memphis, Tennessee. *The Great Jug Bands* (The Origin Jazz Library, 4).
"On the Road Again," September 11, 1928, Memphis, Tennessee.
More of That Jug Band Sound (The Origin Jazz Library, 19). This is a particularly fine example of the kazoo working with the harmonica.

"Overseas Stomp," September 13, 1928, place unknown.
The Jug Bands (RF Records,6) and *Jugs, Washboards and Kazoos* (RCA Victor Vintage Series, LPV–540). The first album gives a recording date of 1927.
"Jug Band Waltz," September 15, 1928, Memphis, Tennessee.
The Great Jug Bands (The Origin Jazz Library, 4).
"Whitewash Station," 1928, place unknown. *The Jug Bands* (RF Records, 6). Note Ramey's use of flutter-tonguing in the second break.
"Cocaine Habit," May 17, 1930, Memphis, Tennessee.
The Jug, Jook and Washboard Bands (Blues Classics, 2). "Stonewall Blues," May 17, 1930, Memphis, Tennessee. *The Jug, Jook and Washboard Bands* (Blues Classics, 2).
Walter Taylor's Washboard Band
"Thirty Eight," February 14, 1930, Richmond, Indiana. *The Jug, Jook and Washboard Bands* (Blues Classics, 2). The kazoo is probably played by John Byrd.
Washboard Rhythm Kings
"Brown Skin Mama," no recording date or place. *The Jug, Jook and Washboard Bands* (Blues Classics, 2). The kazoo player is unknown; at one time Jelly Roll Morton played with this band.
The Even Dozen Jug Band (Electra, EKL-246). (A second Even Dozen album contains much of the same material that this first one has.) This band was one of the 1960s revival bands. Josh Rifkin, who does most of the kazoo work, plays in a tone similar to Ben Ramey's (*The Memphis Jug Band*), but without Ramey's easy and relaxed sense of jazz lines. The *Even Dozen* played with a phenomenal hand-trumpet player, Bob Gurland, and Rifkin's playing points up the difference between the kazoo and the horn, whereas Ramey, who worked in a band without a horn, took the horn's place and worked his kazoo against the harmonica.

CHARLES BLACKLOCK

"I was born and raised on a ranch near the small town of Hollister, California. My parents were very poor but we did have an old phonograph and a few records. Also my dad whistled and sang a lot while we worked hard together in the fields. Then when I was in my teens, my dad bought a radio. I remember one program on the radio was called the X-Bar B. Ranch. On this show they played country and cowboy music. They called the musicians the *Cross Cut Boys* and while they were playing music, they would draw a two-man saw through a log. You could hear the steel in the saw sing as they drew it through the log. I always enjoyed music but had very little time to learn. I played a clarinet in a school band for a short time and I fooled with a mandolin for many years."

This is how Charles Blacklock, handsaw player, describes the early years of his life. Things changed for him when one day he heard a man on the radio playing a handsaw, and he knew that was the instrument for him. He studied for a time with Tom Scribner, a professional saw player, and has become well-known himself now. At the age of sixty he is playing for folk festivals, bluegrass festivals and coffee houses, as well as doing some radio work. He is still in California, and presently plays as a guest with the *"Good Ol' Persons"* bluegrass group.

HOW TO MAKE MUSIC ON A HANDSAW
by Charles Blacklock

Beautiful music can be played with a carpenter's handsaw. If you can sing a song or whistle a tune, you can learn to play. The intent of these lessons is to give you a good start toward learning how to play songs or melodies with the saw. The only other thing it should take to become a good saw player is practice. You will find that as you begin to make progress there will be a natural urge to learn more.

Finding the Right Saw

If you don't have a carpenter's saw that seems to be suitable, you can buy a cheap 26-inch saw at the hardware store. A 28- or 30-inch saw is even better. You may wish to purchase one through a music store. They have them listed as tenor and baritone saws. The 28-inch length is the popular one to start with. This is the measurement along the cutting edge.

In the long run you should get nearly two octaves of music from a 28-inch saw. Most carpenter's saws will give you an octave of music. Many will give you an octave and a half. A good carpenter's saw with sufficient length can give you up to two octaves, and saws marked and sold as musical saws will give you up to two octaves.

Starting with a Mallet

You can get a good start toward playing the saw with a small homemade mallet. Before you practice with a bow, learn to play a few notes with a mallet. You can make one with a clothes hanger. Cut a piece of wire from the coat-hanger about 11½ inches long, and bend it to make a mallet about 8 inches long. Tape a little piece of felt material on the mallet end. It will look like the ones shown here.

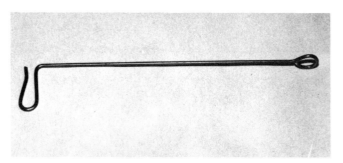 

In the following pages you will learn that you can use this mallet to find the notes on the saw. As you locate the notes, you can mark them, but do not mark your saw until you have read farther on so that you know you are marking it correctly.

If for some reason making the mallet is too much for you, you can use an ordinary pencil and tap along the edge of the saw, although the mallet will give you a more pleasing sound.

Position for Self and Saw

Sit on a solid chair. The chair should be a comfortable height when your feet are in the following positions. Place your left foot flat on the floor. Put your right foot back far enough so that the heel of your right foot does not touch the floor. Place the saw over your left leg with the handle just behind your knee, with the teeth of the saw facing you. Bring your right leg over to hold the saw handle firmly between your legs. Check your position against this picture.

Try not to let the saw blade touch your clothing as it will deaden the sound.

Placing the S-Curve in the Saw

Now you need a slight S-curve in the saw. Do this by grasping the small end of the saw in your left hand and bending lightly with your thumb to make the curve. Check the pictures of the saw held in playing position. It seems that most beginners put too much curve in the saw. You want just a slight S-curve. Keep this slight curve in the saw all the time except for a few high notes. When you have reached the highest note possible with the S-curve in the saw, you may let out the curve and bend the saw down a little farther to reach two or three more notes. Do not try these higher notes until you have learned to play the other ones.

Finding Notes on the Saw

Producing notes on the saw calls for a little co-ordination. You must not only tap the saw in the right place for a given note, but the bend in the saw must be correct for that note also. The following pictures will give you the idea.

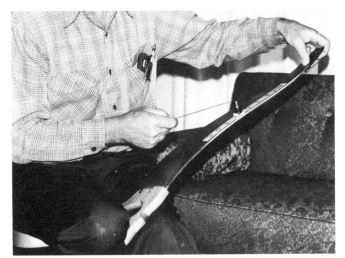

Figure 1

Figure 2

The first figure shows you about where you would find note *F*, and the second about where *A* is located. Look at the differences in both the bend in the saw and the position of the mallet on the saw. Start tapping about 6 inches from the handle of your saw and work your way up, finding the rest of the notes in the same manner.

If you have a piano or other instrument (a harmonica can be quite helpful here if you happen to play), you can compare the sounds you're making with the notes on the other instrument. As you find each note, you might want to use a felt pen to mark them on the saw. This will help you until finding the notes becomes automatic. If you can play a harmonica, this seems to be of some help in comparing the sounds of the notes. The photograph will give you an idea as to about where you will find the notes on the saw. Lower notes are at the handle end, and the higher notes occur where the saw narrows.

Vibrating the Saw

You need to vibrate the saw to bring out the music and to sustain the sound. This can be done with your hand and thumb at the end of the saw, or with your leg on the handle by vibrating with your foot. I prefer the latter method. This is the reason for the heel of your right foot not touching the floor. This is quite hard to do at first, and takes a good deal of practice. After awhile it becomes more automatic, and much easier. You can always keep working at this to obtain the perfected vibrato that you desire.

Once a young lad asked me if it would make me nervous to play for his class at school as the class was large. I assured him not to worry, because nervousness doesn't bother a saw player; it only brings out the proper tremelo needed in the music he is playing.

Practice

Practice at least thirty minutes a day and you will soon be able to play some tunes. If you don't get some notes out of your saw right away, don't get discouraged; just keep trying. When you get the "knack," your saw will all of a sudden start to sing for you.

Bending from Note to Note

When bending your saw blade from note to note with your left hand, do it with a fairly quick movement. This will help to give you better tone quality. When you move from note to note you may not always land on the exact tone you are after, but your ear will let you know and the adjustment can be made fast. After awhile you will automatically find the right note every time.

Remember these tips to produce any given note—the saw blade must have the correct bend, the mallet or bow must hit the right location, and the saw must be vibrating to sustain the note.

In time, playing the saw will be somewhat like whistling. If you know a tune, you'll be able to play it. Of course to arrive at this stage will take time, as the saw is not an easy instrument to learn. It helps to realize that becoming professional may take many years' practice.

If you read music, you'll have the advantage of knowing where the piece can be played on the saw, where the starting note lies and the key the tune should be played in. If you don't read music at all, you'll have to experiment a little, and it may take you a bit longer to learn the piece. Even if you do read music, you should still listen to how others play the piece when playing with other instruments.

Playing along with a Record

While learning, try playing along with a record recorded in a key that fits within the range of your saw. You'll discover that you have to do a lot of extra practice to produce the low notes and the very high notes. The easiest notes to play on a tenor saw are the notes from D to D.

Playing with a Bow

When you have found enough notes with the mallet and have your technique down fairly

well, you can start using the bow.

Use a good heavy bow (the cello bow is ideal) and tighten it quite a bit more than you would for playing a stringed instrument. Also keep it well coated with rosin at all times. Use a good grade of rosin. You can purchase it at any music store, and it's pronounced "rahzin." Work some rosin into the hair at the ends of the bow, and then work it in across the rest of the bow so as to distribute it evenly. To "work it in" means to rub it along the length of the strings of the bow. Do not put your fingers on the hair of the bow or along the back edge of the saw at any time, as the oil or moisture from your fingers will ruin the effects of the rosin.

Bowing Methods

There are several methods used in bowing the saw. This next one is the method I find best for playing melodies, and for solo playing. First, though, you'll need to ready the bow for playing. You don't want to tighten the bow excessively, yet tighten it much more than you would for playing a stringed instrument. You may have to find a string player among your friends and get some help with this, or ask at a music store.

Hold the bow as shown here.

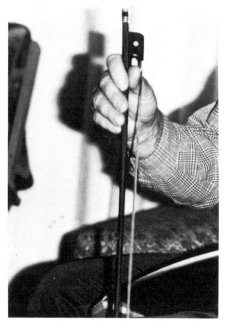

Notice how the thumb is placed between the hair and the back of the bow, with the rest of your fingers down the back of the bow.

Now position your saw and try for a note with the bow. Bow the back edge of the saw with a lively stroke. Make sure the teeth of the saw are toward you, and do not put the bow against the teeth of the saw! Use short strokes. Each stroke needs to be only about one inch long with a considerable amount of pressure against the back edge of the saw. As time goes on, you may want to use longer strokes according to the volume and effect you desire. This could mean bowing two to three inches or even a little more at times. Use both up and down strokes in accordance with timing and convenience while playing. There are a few situations where drawing the bow lightly across the saw for a considerable length, sometimes for the full length of the bow, is desireable—for example, when playing with other instruments and bowing high notes which are hard to sustain, even with a lot of vibration. In this case, draw the bow lightly across the saw to sustain the note.

These next four pictures show where to bow certain key notes on the saw. You can locate the other notes between these.

Figure 5

Figure 6

Figure 3 is about where you will find lower D. Figure 4 is where you find F. Figure 5 is A, and Figure 6 is about where you will get the higher D.

Don't forget to loosen the bow a little when storing it away.

Care of the Saw

Keep your saw blade clean. I use powdered pumice, which you can get from the hardware store. Sprinkle some onto the blade and rub it with a soft cloth. Each day, rub off any finger prints that you may have made on your saw blade. If you don't keep the saw blade wiped clean, it will soon turn a dark color and rust quickly wherever fingerprints are left. One saw player I know uses pumice in the rock form. A clean saw produces a better tone.

Having the Bow Rehaired

If your bow is old, you may need to have it rehaired. After a few years of playing, you will notice the difference between a freshly rehaired bow and one in which the hair has been worn out. Horse hair has little barbs on it that seem to help hold the rosin in. As these barbs wear out, you spend more and more time rosining your bow. You don't need to have hair missing on the bow to know that it may be worn out.

When having a bow rehaired, consider using black horse hair, as it is somewhat coarser than white. This difference can improve your sound. Call your local music store to find out where you can restore your bow.

Saw Lore

When you play a saw, it is nice to know a little bit about saw "lore." For instance, the length of the saw is the measurement of the blade along the teeth side. A rip saw or a cross-cut saw can be determined by the shape of the teeth—the rip saw has larger teeth for tearing or ripping the wood, and a cross-cut saw has smaller, finer teeth. An eight- or ten-point saw, etc. is referring to the number of teeth per inch. Both are fine for making music.

Because of the many questions that are asked of a saw player, you should know about the steel that your saw is made of. For example, is it Swedish steel? Some companies tell you what alloys are in the steel; for instance, silver steel is steel containing 2% silver.

Other Tips and Observations

When other musicians are playing with you, or you are playing with accompaniment, if possible sit with the others on your right, or sit at such an angle that you can hear them clearly. If you are not seated this way, you will find that due to the angle of the saw, the sounds you produce tend to block the music to your left, making it harder to play together.

When entertaining small groups of people, tell them about your saw and bow. Point out that saw players class their instruments as tenors, high tenors, and baritones, and so on. And it is always interesting to mention that the bow is strung with real horse hair.

Demonstrate to your audience how they too, can learn to play their own hand saw. To do this, play a short tune by tapping the saw with a pencil or mallet. This showmanship adds to the entertainment and your friends' enjoyment.

If you happen to be a bashful person, loosen up by contacting other saw players in your area. You will discover some interesting people, as well as new styles and methods of playing. By practicing the lessons presented in this book and seeing firsthand what others do, you'll pick up ideas that will help you develop a pleasing style of your own.

Observing Other Saw Players

Of all the saw players that I know, or have watched and heard, I have only seen a few who shared the same style or sound. This is probably a good thing, as it shows just how much individuality and variety you can put into your saw playing.

Of the six professional saw players that I have watched, four hold and handle the bow in a very similar fashion to the way I do. Two of them grasp the bow somewhere near midpoint, and seem to use "Up" strokes only. Some of them use their hands rather than the foot and knee to vibrate the saw.

Finally, let me stress strongly that a saw does not have to be marked as a musical saw to be a good one. I recently ran into one that a carpenter was using which was an excellent tenor saw. And one professional saw player that I met played a carpenter's saw for many years, and it equals any saw sold as an instrument.

Now that you have learned this much don't stop here. Even professional saw players of many years experience continue to learn and improve through the years.

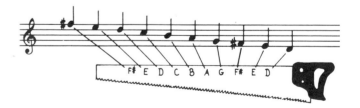

Reading Tablature on Tunes for the Musical Saw

F♯ D C D E F♯ G A B C̄ D̄ E̅ F̅
Low   Middle (with no lines)   High

HOME ON THE RANGE

RED RIVER VALLEY

LEN MAC EACHRON

Photo by Bob Cooper

Little did the author's mother think when she gave birth to her second son in Techow, Shantung, China, back in 1919 that he would grow up to plague the folk music world with an article about nose flutes. So she carelessly brought him back to the United States in 1923 and let things take their course. After proceeding through the usual childhood diseases—piano, trombone, and so on—he went off to college about ten blocks from home in Oberlin, Ohio, and there he got a reluctant AB in Economics thus further throwing the wary off the scent of things to come.

After five years in the army during World War II came the big debate about how to spend his share of the GI Bill. In the meantime he had lured an unsuspecting Suanna Manley (Su for short) into becoming his bride. Together they finally agreed that he would try a semester in law school at the University of Illinois, and after he flunked out (everyone knows how tough law school is), he would become an industrial arts teacher. As luck would have it, he did not flunk out and ended up practicing patent law for about twenty years.

As a result of a series of events too incredible to be fiction, he finally became the head of a small company manufacturing folk-type instruments. He has twice been the judge of a "Mouth Off" contest of performances on all types of mouth and head resonator instruments, including the nose flute. In addition, he plays the nose flute with enough facility to distort the judgment of many people who go into his shop, and has hence sold a goodly number of the instruments. He therefore modestly admits that with the possible exceptions of the nose flute inventors, Davis and Berry, their respective patent attorneys and a handful of high priests in the South Pacific, there is no one better qualified to blur the facts about the nose flute than he.

HOW TO FIND AND LEARN TO PLAY THE NOSE FLUTE
by Len Mac Eachron

If you are a buff of murky history, the next few paragraphs are just your speed. If you are eager to get playing, however, and are of the "history can wait" school, skip down to the heading on "Playing."

To judge by standard reference works, the nose flute, like the jaw harp,[1] has a rather long, shadowy (but not illicit) past. About the only information one can easily find is that nose flutes are old, and were one of two musical instruments[2] used by the Sakai Tribe of the north central inland portion of the Malay Peninsula. It is casually said that other tribes also used nose flutes, but the Sakai is the only tribe mentioned by name. This much from the Encyclopedia Brittanica and Webster's New International Dictionary.

If you are willing to run down two books by Sybil Marcuse, however, you can uncover all sorts of fascinating information, if of somewhat limited application. For example, you can discover the list of some fifty-eight different names for the nose flute. "Lantoy" is the name used by the Batoks of Palawan. (I have not researched to learn the location of Palawan.) The Polynesians are said to call their nose flutes "Fango-fango." You may be enlightened to learn that in Asia the flutes are found exclusively off-shore from the Nicobar Island and that the Congolese have a nose flute which has no finger holes. The pitch of the tones is varied by more or less covering the lower end of the flute.[3] (The lower end is the one remote from the point of blowing.) You can read that the nose flute occurs in Europe "only in Macedonia except for the ubiquitous sheet metal toy." Marcuse reports that the Polynesians use only the right nostril while the Melanesians use only the left. In most cultures where it appears, however, the nose flute is a religious and mystical fertility symbol. The air from the nostril was thought to carry the soul . . . not to be confused with soul music or Seoul music. But the most important and useful information to be derived from all this research is that the "mother-load," so to speak, of nose flute history and folk lore is in the South Pacific. Armed with this information, one could draft an appeal to the foundation for the preservation of the primitive arts, or whatever, and arrange a study program on the site in the South Pacific. It could reasonably start about the first of December and run. . . .

How to Find a Nose Flute

Enough of the history, incomplete though it may be. What we are mainly interested in is how to spot and learn to play the modern version of the traditional nose flute . . . the one referred to by Marcuse as the "ubiquitous sheet metal toy." What we presently call the nose flute is a delightfully small and hence marvelously portable instrument. It is also an extremely simple instrument requiring very little in the way of manual dexterity. Nowadays, they are molded from plastic rather than being made from sheet metal and are somewhat fragile, a fact that tends to build a rather satisfactory re-sale market. It is known in the trade as the "Humanatone," and can be purchased at most music stores.

Every one of these units that I have seen has been made from red plastic, but I doubt that any reliable political significance can be deduced from this fact. On the other hand, its low cost (35¢ or less even in these inflated times) tends to make it assume the character of the universally affordable, hence "working man's" instrument. Its super-portability also lends itself to its owner being "on the lam" as we used to say years ago, or in the underground as they now refer to it. In spite of the above facts, it is clear that the national distributor of the Humanatone is not a conduit for "red" propaganda, regardless of its subtlety. We can safely assume and assert, therefore, without fear of reasonable contradiction, that the red of the modern nose flute is the red of the RED, WHITE and BLUE.

Playing the Nose Flute

We have reached that exciting moment, and you will now find that the nose flute is both difficult and simple to play. Occasionally someone finds it difficult or impossible to exhale only through the nose. These people find that attempting to play the nose flute is pure, unadulterated frustration. Those with heavy beards and moustaches also have air leak problems that can turn out to be more than they can handle. For the balance of humanity, and let us hope that you, dear reader, are in this group, playing the instrument might be said to be a breeze.

The readily available, plastic Humanatone brand nose flute has a small upper portion that more or less fits the lower end of the human nose. When this upper flared portion is pressed against the lower end of the nose, air being exhaled through the nostrils is directed down a passageway to a fipple structure (as in the recorder, tin whistle or other flagolet.) This fipple structure centers in a larger, lower flared portion designed to cover the mouth. When the air passing the fipple divides, the air in the mouth is set in motion, as in other end-blown flutes, and a tone is emitted. As the size (or shape or something) of the resonating cavity is altered, the pitch of the tone changes.

Very simply . . . blow only through your nostrils! Hold the nose flute between your thumb and forefinger. Press firmly against your nose and mouth, and be sure to keep your mouth *open*. Make sure there are no air leaks.

There are at least two ways to alter the effective size of the oral cavity, or mouth, as we folk people are inclined to refer to it. One can make his cheeks move, ranging from puckering up in a kiss-like arrangement, to pulling the cheeks back in a foolish grin. The other way to vary the volume of air space in the mouth is to position the tongue in a variety of ways, each of which will produce a change in the pitch of the sound emitted by the nose flute. It is well nigh impossible to say just where the tongue should be placed to produce a G or an A, because some people have bigger mouths than others. (This we all know from sad experience.) A little experimenting, however, soon will allow anyone who has success at all to begin to be able to repeat a series of notes . . . and that's really what music is.

One of the easier things to practice on, and thereby both learn to play the flute and gain community recognition (if not respect) is bugle calls. This is true of all the mouth (oral cavity to all you medics, pedants, and patent lawyers) resonator instruments. These include the jaw harp and mouth bow, as well as the modern nose flute. I have been told that the relative ease of the bugle calls has something to do with the notes of the calls being the principal harmonies of the basic note of the instrument. As the principal harmonies are more pronounced in sound, they are more easily found than the other harmonics. Once you have mastered a few bugle calls, you should be able to go on to the simpler folk melodies.

Versatility of the Nose Flute

Actually the nose flute is more versatile than the other mouth resonator instruments. The reason for this is easily understood. By changing the effective size of your mouth cavity when playing a nose flute, you are doing something akin to putting your fingers on and off the holes of a fingered flute. As one removes fingers from the finger holes of a flagolet, the tube, for tone purposes, is shortened, or made smaller. The reverse is true as the fingers are placed over the finger holes. As the inventor of the Humanatone says in his patent, the device has a range limited only by the anatomy of the player. Thus a soprano with a big mouth might be able to play very low notes, while a small mouth bass could only hit high tones. Mr. E. W. Davis, for that is the inventor's name, also claims that a range of three octaves can be achieved with a little practice. I, for one, have never been able to get three octaves, but believe I have come fairly close to two. It is enough range in any case, to play lots of folk tunes. Ones like "Boil That Cabbage Down," "Railroad Bill," and "Cripple Creek" are a lead pipe cinch.

Mr. Davis does provide one very clear improvement over the sheet metal unit (disclosed by Berry in his earlier patent, and I presume the one referred to by Marcuse) which is a tremolo hole (aperture to you patent lawyers) in the mouth covering portion of the Humanatone. This hole when covered and uncovered with a finger, produces a slight variation in the pitch of the note being produced. By covering and uncovering the hole rapidly, a tremolo is made, the speed of which is limited only by the dexterity of the player.

Thoughts on Protecting Your Nose Flute

As mentioned earlier, the plastic nose flute breaks quite easily when sat upon or banged against a hard object or used as a pad between you and your shoulder belt in the car. It has even been known to crack when jammed too hard against a nose. This should not be confused with jamming it against a hard nose. In fact, a hard nose is very valuable in getting past the early stages of ridicule that sometimes precede one's rise to the concert stage. The breakage problem can be solved in several ways. The wealthy may be inclined to keep several on hand and treat them as disposable. Others have been known to repair them with masking tape.

A third possibility is to manipulate the thumb and/or other digits to substitute for missing portions of the nose receiving part. This third solution has the hidden merit of offering a ready excuse for a middling to weak performance. It also suggests you have had a heavy concert schedule and simply have not had time to pick up a new one. Still another approach that depends at least partly on luck, is to find one of the old sheet metal units that are a considerably hardier breed.[4]

Finally, one can make a hardshell case for his or her nose flute or flutes. Any appropriately deep, small jewelry box or the like will do, metal being the preferred material. To receive the plastic nose flute, the box you need must be at least 2 cm. (about $^{13}/_{16}$ inch) by 6.25 cm. ($2^7/_{16}$) by 6.75 cm. ($2^{11}/_{16}$ inch). It may, of course, be larger, and should be if you plan to carry two or more units at once.

Some Final Thoughts on the Nose Flute

Well, that is about it except for a passing bit of philosophy that may help you over those early hurdles on your way to the big time.

If you would succeed as a nose flutist you need to consider your reflective occular (with apologies to Gilbert and Sullivan and anyone for whom that ruins Yeoman of the Guard.) In short, NEVER LOOK IN A MIRROR TO SEE IF YOU ARE DOING IT RIGHT! If you see how weird you look with that thing against your nose, you are apt to give it up, then and there.

Remember that when you first play the nose flute for the immature, it is possible that they may laugh. It is not easy to stay cool in the face of raucous laughter. You can do several things under these circumstances. You can become the Victor Borge of the nose flute. This is a particularly good idea if a substantial portion of the laughter is 6 foot, 4 inch, 250 pound laughter. The other thing you can do is to remember that there are not that many laughs for most people in this old world, and be glad that you lightened some person's burden . . . if only for a moment. Good luck!

Notes

1. In Yugoslavia the jaw harp is called a drombulje, and Mike Cooney tells me that the Dutch call it the Youngster's Harp or Juggen Harfe.
2. The other instrument that the Sakai use or used was said to be a rude lute, which I would dearly love to have. Imagine the sensation of announcing, ". . . and now I will play 'Go Tell Aunt Rhody' on my rude lute."
3. It is interesting to note that there is a flute made in Norway that has fipple arrangement but no finger holes. The lower end of the flute is left opened or covered to provide two ranges of notes. Within each range, five to six notes can be played by over-blowing to give a total of ten to twelve notes. The "scale" produced in this way is roughly equivalent to the Mixolydian scale on the dulcimer.
4. If you have no luck finding one of the sheet metal units, but have a modicum of sheet metal fabrication skill, you might make yourself one according to the patent issued by Berry (see Bibliography). You can get a copy of this patent from the Commissioner of Patents, United States Patent Office, Arlington, Virginia. At the writing of this chapter, a U.S. Patent copy cost 59¢.

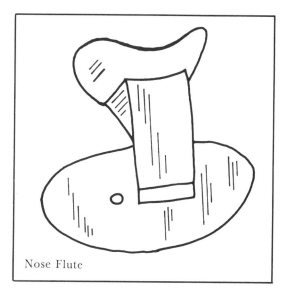

Nose Flute

Bibliography

Webster's New International Dictionary, second edition, 1934.

Encyclopedia Brittanica, 14th Edition, Vol. 14, p. 714.

Grove's Dictionary of Music and Musicians, 5th Edition, Eric Blom, Ed., St. Martin's Press, Inc., 1954 (see Folk Music, Yugoslavia.)

Marcuse, Sybil, *A Comprehensive Dictionary of Music*, Doubleday and Co., Inc., 1964.

Marcuse, Sybil, *A Survey of Musical Instruments*, Doubleday and Co., Inc., 1964.

Skeat and Blogden, *Pagan Tribes of the Malay Peninsula*, 1906.

US Patent #2,197,993 to C.M. Berry, for Vocamonica, April 23, 1940.

US Patent #2,245,432 to E.W. Davis, for Musical Instrument, June 10, 1941.

PETER MENTA

Born in New Haven, Connecticut, and escaping to Fordham University for a college career, Peter Menta was drawn home again to the good folk music in his home town. A very fine drummer, Peter found himself also fascinated with the possibilities of playing some of his drum techniques on the washboard, and has become a popular washboard player in the state. He has "jammed on the board," as he phrases it, with Sonny Terry and Brownie McGhee, and the *Basin St. Five Dixieland Band.*

For about a year and a half, Peter took on the responsibility of being executive director for the Exit Coffee House. Along with all this he was working with several bands. He was previously a member of the *Golden Nectar Good-time Band*, and the *Blake Street Gut Band.* Now he is playing washboard, drums and harmonica with the *Ten Years Late Band*, as well as playing harmonica and washboard with *Homesick John O'Leary.* He made an E.P. record with "Homesick," playing harmonica.

He's been recorded on two other albums, one by the *Golden Nectar Band*, and the other, presently available recorded with the *Ten Years Late Band*, and it's called *Bootleg Blues.* This recording was made live at the Theater in the Space, a coffee house in New Haven. And to top it all off, he's currently the musical director for two night clubs in the same city.

HOW TO MAKE AND PLAY A WASHBOARD
by Peter Menta

The very first time I ever heard a washboard being played was on a record by Jim Kweskin and his band. Much of the rhythmic drive of the group came from the board, expertly played by a tremendous blues musician, Geoff Muldaur. So I went out and bought myself a tin washboard, little realizing that I was becoming part of a time honored musical tradition.

As a musical instrument, the washboard probably dates back at least to the turn of the century. People more than likely discovered the percussive possibilities of this household utensil while sitting around in their kitchens making music. Someone wanting to make some rhythm on something may well have picked up the washboard and found it had a very inspiring sound.

Harold Coulander in his book *Negro Folk Music* suggests that the use of a scraping device had its roots in Africa, perhaps in the form of a gourd or jawbone. In Cuba we have the "guiro," a notched gourd, which is scraped with a wire or a piece of bamboo. Today it has become one of the most popular rhythm instruments in Latin American music. Whatever its pre-American ancestry was, we do know that by the 1920s the washboard was an important instrument in that glorious musical hybrid . . . the jug band. Poor Southerners picked up, or invented, instruments like the jug, kazoo, washtub bass and the harmonica, and played blues, ragtime and the popular tunes of the day.

By the 1930s, jug band music was a commercial musical entity, and one group called the *Memphis Jug Band*, who remained together for about seven years, sold quite a few records. On these early cuts you can hear some skillful washboard playing and you can distinguish the fact that there were attachments on the boards. By the late 1930s washboard technique had become quite refined and polished on the recordings of "novelty" pop and jazz bands. Such groups as the *Washboard Rhythm Kings*, *The*

Five Harmaniacs, the *Hoosier Hot Shots*, Tiny Parkham and Spike Jones often featured complex washboard solos, frequently by the drummer of the group. There was one solo washboard player, however, whose name stands out in the history of the blues. He was undoubtedly the best known and most widely recorded washboard artist, and his name was Robert Brown, better known as "Washboard Sam."

Originally from Arkansas, Sam was in Chicago by the early 1930s recording for the RCA Bluebird Label. Many of these records featured the guitar work of Big Bill Broonzy, who claimed Sam was his half-brother. Sam's singing and playing soon became one of the most popular sounds on the Bluebird label. He recorded almost one hundred and fifty sides, many of which featured piano, trumpet, sax and bass. Sam also played dates with other blues musicians in and around Chicago, among them the great Delta musician Bukka White.

Whether working with a slide guitarist or a big band combo, Sam's sound was immediately recognizable. His style was very basic, driving and intense, and he used simple syncopations which really made the music swing. Sam was a "blues" washboard player. He used thimbles on most of his fingers, and was gifted with a strong voice, which he needed to rise above the clamorous sound of the washboard. He attached a phonograph turntable to the board for a cymbal, and I would venture to guess that he may have even listened to Gene Krupa records to get ideas for soloing.

Washboard accompaniment was also prevalent on the recordings of another extremely popular blues artist, Blind Boy Fuller, as well as on the recordings of Sonny Terry and Brownie McGhee.

By the late 1940s a new style was becoming popular in the blues field. The down home sound of Muddy Waters, Howling Wolf, and Elmore James was what people were looking for. These musicians required a heavier punch in their sound, so the drums became dominant in the new rhythm and blues. In the world of commercial recording, the washboard's popularity waned, and then was brought back in the early 60s as the Jug Band revival took place. Groups like Jim Kweskin's, Dave Van Ronk's *Jug Stompers*, and the *Even Dozen Jug Band*, all used and recorded with a washboard. The only group I can think of today who is using a washboard is the *Nitty Gritty Dirt Band* . . . and the more power to them for keeping it going!

How to Put Your Own Washboard Together

Now at this point all you aspiring washboard players are probably quite anxious to find out how to set up your own washboard. So let's get down to business. . . . Go down to your local hardware store or junk dealer and buy a metal washboard. You've heard of the National steel guitar; well, they make the National washboard, too. You might try several before you buy one, because some have a better "clack" than others. Keep in mind that the heavier the metal on the washboard, the fatter, fuller and less tinny the sound will be. My own is made from two washboards bound together with foam rubber padding in between. Each one is made from a different kind of metal, giving me two different tones. If you can find a washboard made of zinc, rather than tin or aluminum, it will be more durable and have a fuller sound.

Many players use attachments on their boards to vary the sound. Let your imagination run wild. People have tried everything from cowbells, woodblocks, pots and pans, bells, pipes, triangles and cheese graters to a Boy Scout mess kit! One of the most interesting effects I've heard of was produced by a fellow named Hezzie Trietsch, who played in the group called the *Hoosier Hot Shots* in the 1940s. He rigged up about ten bicycle horns to his board, each tuned to a different note, and he played melodies on them during his solo time. A Chinese frying pan, called a Wok, also makes a great cymbal. One time, at an outdoor concert I hung a Wok from a tree branch and played it as part of my solo. The natural food buffs in the audience loved it!

Thimbles for Your Fingers

The next step is to secure some metal thimbles at the local sewing supply shop, or even the local Five-and-Ten. Outfit as many of your fingers as you plan to use. I usually play with thimbles on the three largest fingers, and the thumbs of each hand—eight altogether. That will get you maximum volume from the board.

In choosing your thimbles be a little fussy. They just don't make them as well as they used to, so try to find the heaviest ones you can. The heavier the metal, the better the sound. They come in different sizes, so be sure they fit well and snugly on each finger, so that at the peak of some incredible solo you may be playing, they won't go flying off into the audience.

Of course, playing with thimbles is not the only way it is done. Some folks use rings, wires, nails, drumsticks, or their own fingers. Julie Hovey, who played with a Dixieland group called the *Galvinized Washboard Band*, set the board in her lap and used heavy metal soup spoons. Although she played only one side of the board, her techniques were the same: tapping and scraping.

Positions for Holding the Washboard

When it comes to finding the right position to hold the washboard for playing, the rule is "different strokes for different folks." I play mine upside down and perpendicular to me, attaching it around my neck and waist with belts. The left hand can then play the left side and the right hand the right side. This technique enables me to stand up and move around while playing. And we've already mentioned Julie Hovey, who holds hers in her lap. Experiment with what feels best for you.

Playing the Washboard

Assuming you have a basic sense of rhythm, let's start with some simple patterns. You will use two different attacks while playing—a tap and a scrape. Let's begin with a basic 1–2 rhythm. (If you play the guitar it would be like a Carter strum: thumb, brush.) Tap the left side of the board with your left hand, and then scrape the right side—a short scrape. Count: tap . . . 1 and scrape . . . 2. Practice this rhythm until it comes easily and naturally. You can also reverse the tap, scrape motion if you like.

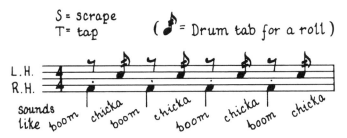

After you have this pattern down, substitute a scraping motion for the tap so that both hands are scraping the basic 1–2. Now, alternate between both of these patterns. Keep in mind that the direction of the scraping, either upward or downward, and the angle with which the thimbles strike the washboard, will have different effects on the sound. I have developed a style of playing by embellishing the basic motions with variations. The patterns that I use most frequently are diagrammed. Most of these are based on alternating eighth and sixteenth note patterns, similar to the role of the cymbal in a swing or blues band. Try practicing with your favorite records.

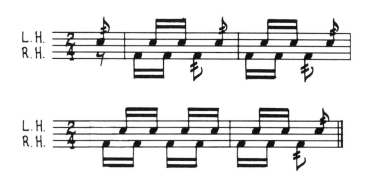

Playing with Others

After practicing with records it will be fun to get together with some friends and see how you make out playing live music. When playing music with other people, you are first and foremost a time keeper, and your duty is to make the music swing. If you start playing too busily, you may detract from the overall sound. This is a common mistake that beginners on any instrument may make. At it's best, the washboard provides a light rhythmic drive, without being too heavy and ponderous. Many folk, country and Dixieland musicians tend to favor the washboard player and enjoy having a good one sit in with them.

Playing Solos

Now you are ready for a solo flight. Everyone loves to hear the washboard player take a solo, and this is your chance to really express yourself and stretch out. When doing a solo, keep in mind that you are primarily a rhythm instrument; so keep the beat going, vary the patterns of tapping and scraping, and use whatever attachments you may have. You can pick up lots of ideas for solos by listening to drummers. Remember that some of the finest washboard players were also drummers . . . but a fine washboard player can also be one who never played another instrument before. So swing!

And So Forth

There are really no definitive schools of washboard playing. Like most folk instruments it is learned by ear, through practicing the basics and listening to records, and passed on from one person to another. Although its origins are makeshift, it has succeeded in captivating many an audience, and appeared on countless recordings. Hopefully, its values will continue to be appreciated.

In the meantime, best of luck to you as a washboard player, and remember that you don't have to rely on electricity to make music or keep your clothes clean!

Discography

This list is by no means complete as a catalog of washboard music. Some of the records may be out of print, but you may write to the record companies directly and ask if they still have them in stock.

Blues Classics by the Jug, Jook, and Washboard Bands
Arhoolie Records, Box 9195, Berkeley, California. This record has several different bands doing jug band and blues tunes with washboard, including a great Washboard Sam number called "Bucket's Got a Hole in It."

Bukka White, Parchman Farm
Columbia C30036
Classic Delta blues with Washboard Sam sitting in.
Jim Kweskin and the Jug Band and *Jug Band Music*
Vanguard VRS 9139 or VSD 2158
The first two albums feature washboard work by Geoff Muldaur.
Feelin' Lowdown, Washboard Sam
RCA Vintage Series LPV 577
"The Bluebird Beat" with Big Bill and Memphis Slim
Jugs, Washboards and Kazoos
RCA Vintage Series LPV 540
Pick up this incredible record. Excellent washboard work by one Ernie Marrero with The Tiny Parkham Band and H. Smith with *The Washboard Rhythm Kings*.
There is also a great record that came out on the Chess label a while back, and it features Sam and Big Bill, but chances are it's out of print. If you see it anywhere, grab it! It has some great solo work by Washboard Sam.

DON DWORKIN

Don Dworkin (second from left) and friends.

Don Dworkin was born twenty-six years ago in Buffalo, N.Y., a place heretofor famous for being the hometown of Millard Fillmore and prefabricated snowdrifts. He went through an uneventful childhood and even more uneventful puberty. However, this phase passed, and he soon discovered his first true love . . . the washtub bass. Beginning in high school and continuing until now, he has been partially responsible for unleashing a series of semifamous, legendarily obscure jug, skiffle and string bands upon the East Coast. Some of these oft-forgotten bands include the *South Happiness St. Society Skiffle Band*, the *Zing Kings Jug Band*, *Star Spangled Washboard Band*, *Pullin' Teeth* and his current ensemble, *The Spongey Delights* (as pictured). The *Spongey Delights* are a further note up the evolutionary scale and play an ecclectic mixture of 30s jazz, old-time fiddle music, bluegrass, country, contemporary and original folk, and ever-popular Gregorian chants.

Don now does most of his music on the stand-up bass fiddle, but for years practiced his special form of insanity on the washtub bass, sometimes known as the gut-bucket, the one-string, or the thumper. He also plays washboard, jug, jaw harp, spoons, and when coaxed into it, a mean hand of old maid. He lists his main influences as Fritz Richmond (of Jim Kweskin's *Jug Band*), Jesse "The Lone Cat" Fuller, Fats Waller, Spike Jones, Anita Bryant, the *Monroe Brothers*, and *Dr. Jazz and the Ukelele Ladies*.

HOW TO MAKE AND PLAY THE WASHTUB BASS
by Don Dworkin

To me, jug band music has always represented the marriage of good-time music, off-the-wall humor and simplified fun instrumentation. It is not unusual to find the typical jug band made up of guitar, banjo, washboard, washtub bass, spoons, jug and kazoos, playing such diverse musical styles as ragtime, rock, and Broadway show tunes. Each jug band you find is an original, using the rhythmical, colorful instruments as an excuse to express its own personality. What counts most is not the musical virtuosity, but the spirit in which tunes are played.

Generally found holding together such zany gatherings is the beat of the washtub bass, a homemade instrument as diverse in its methods of construction as in the styles of music it is generally found playing. What follows will be the way that I've decided to put mine together, a method defined and refined through a decade of flumping the old gut-bucket. But first, a short though poignant history.

The washtub bass owes its origins to Africa, where its ancester was the earth bow. This consisted of a shallow hole dug next to a sapling tree, an animal skin stretched over the hole, and then connected to the top of the sapling by a long animal sinew. Not exactly portable, but great if you're into organic music. Accompanying such jam sessions were instruments such as the gourd and the equivalent forerunner of the banjo. After Africans became American slaves,

45

some traditions were saved, and the African influence has indeed been the base for most of the music that's originated in America.

Central to early jazz was the sound of the jug band, a highly rhythmical percussive amalgamation. The earthbow became the washtub bass, and the gourd, the washboard, and the four-string banjo developed into the modern tenor sound, with guitars, comb and paper, kazoos and jugs further coloring the effect. Jug bands had their heyday in the 1920s, and again in the revival of the 1960s; they still survive in such underground music centers as the New York City Subway.

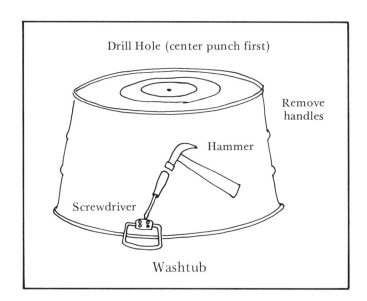

Construction of the Washtub Bass

The three main components you are going to need to construct the washtub bass are a washtub, a pole, and a string. Necessary incidentals are an eyebolt, washers and nuts.

If you are either lucky or resourceful, you can find a washtub in your Aunt Nelly's basement or at "Nick's Antiques" in that slightly shady neighborhood downtown. If not, you can make like every other perspiring bass player and travel to a well-stocked hardware store that carries round, galvanized steel washtubs. The tub will most likely represent your major expense, about six to seven dollars. The brand to look for is Wheeling Steel or Reeves, but stay away from American Hardware and Sears. These should clearly be your second choice, since they tend to be brittle and give way more easily to the constant pull-pressure of the string. A #2 size tub is the size I use for a good range of notes; for that real low-down and dirty sound, try a #3.

Next you'll have to remove the two handles on the sides of the tub using a handle and screwdriver. (If left on, it'll sound more like you're playing maracas than a bass. Drive the screwdriver into the middle of the piece that holds the handle on; twist it until it lifts away from the tub. Remove the handles and gently pound the handle holders flush with the tub.

When this task is complete either drill a hole in the center of the tub top, or in lieu of a drill, knock a large spike or nail through, twist it around and file down the edges of the wound you've created. Be sure the hole is not much larger than the eyebolt.

Now that you have this over-sized cereal bowl with a hole in the bottom, you'll want to beg, borrow, purchase or construct the pole. I use a hardwood pole an inch square and four feet long with the edges smoothly sanded; a rake handle or a broom-stick minus the broom also work well (but of course, I'm not one to make sweeping comparisons). In the flat end on the pole, cut a notch which will fit the lip of the tub. At the top end of the pole, drill the hole in which you will soon attach the string. (Rake handles already have a hole in the end.)

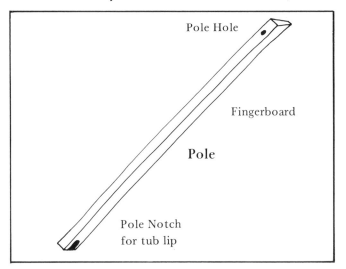

Finally, the string that affords the clearest, cleanest sound is a cat-gut "G" string for an accoustic bass. This can cost around five bucks. For the sake of austerity, or for spares, buy ten to twelve feet of nylon-wrapped curtain cord. This won't be as strong as the gut, and will not sustain the notes as long, but generally gives a satisfactory noise when struck. But watch out . . . it will tend to break if you're continually reaching for those high notes.

Now you have the main materials and have completed the bulk of the physical labor required. The eyebolt, washers and nuts you are going to use to connect the string to the tub. These are set up as shown in the diagram.

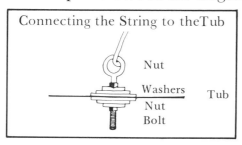

Connecting the String to theTub

Nut

Washers — Tub

Nut
Bolt

Tie one end of the string to the eyebolt and thread the other end through the hole on the opposite end of the pole. Make a good strong knot in this. Now, when you pull it tight it should make an 90° angle with the tub.

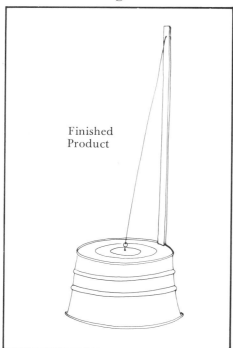

Finished Product

Playing the Tub

As for method, I find that a combination of simultaneously fretting the string and pulling the pole works best for me. It allows a certain freedom in sliding into a note, which is characteristic of the tub bass sound . . . the classic "boing." Make sure that you press down firmly on the string in relation to the fingerboard as you either slap or pluck the notes to fill the bottom of the sound. I can't tell you what notes to play, because you just have to hear them. Your best bet is to play along with records until it begins to sound right. You should also wear gloves (heavy work-type) on one or both hands if you want them to survive. Placing a notched piece of wood or some similar object under one side of the tub is also helpful in allowing the full sound to escape.

By all means, if something else works better, sounds better, or looks better . . . do it! Improvise and improve. Speaking of looking better, you can give the instrument a bit of your personality by splashing some colors or decals on it. Or for those of you who like the rustic look, you can let it rust.

The washtub bass is an instrument that though subtle in tone (boing?) is not physically easy to play. You might even begin to work up a sweat on a good night . . . a great way to get rid of that excess body weight. It's also been known to cause fewer cavities than the high-priced spread, will not cause "ring around the collar," and is a great gift for weddings, anniversaries, and Bar Mitzvahs. So have fun with it!

Discography

Jim Kweskin and the Jug Band
Vanguard VRS 9139 and VSD 2158
Jug Band Music
Vanguard VRS 3159
Garden of Joy
Reprise 6266
Martin, Bogan and Armstrong
Rounder 2003 "Barnyard Dance" and "Flying Fish"
Nitty Gritty Dirt Band
Liberty LST 7507
Jim Kweskin, Good Old Days
Vanguard VSD 19728
See Reverse Side for Title
Vanguard VSD 79234
The Jug Bands
Folkways RF Records 6

RED JONES

Photo by Bob Clark

Hailing from down Virginia way, Red Jones was caught up in the *Kingston Trio* music of the 60s. This was his introduction to folk music, and he was one of many who learned to play the guitar. But what happened after that led him into the world of jug band music, and on to becoming a very talented musician. The jug band music which inspired him was from shows which he saw at summer camp, and several years later he became more involved after hearing *Jim Kweskin* and the *Jug Band*. He found himself forming jug bands (about one a month, he says) that were very informal and just for fun. He logged in most of his jug band experience out in Richmond, Virginia, where he became part of a jug band that had more guitar players than you could shake a stick at. He was chosen to be the one most likely to learn all the "pick-up" instruments: the jug, washboard, bones, tub bass, spoons, bomb shell, and so on. And so began a long-term love affair which is still going on.

Red has travelled all across the country playing bars and clubs wherever he could find work. At the present time he has settled down in Norfolk, Virginia where he teaches guitar, dobro and mandolin, as well as jug band pick-up instruments. You can find him there at Ramblin' Conrad's Guitar Shop and Folklore Center.

HOW TO MAKE MUSIC ON A JUG
by Red Jones

Jug bands, jook bands, washboard bands, "hamfat," skiffle bands, spasm bands. . . . Depending on what part of the South you were in you might have heard any one of these names given to a band. Local musicians in Memphis might not know that their skiffle bands would be called spasm bands in New Orleans, but everyone knew what a jug band was. During the 1920s all over the south, these small breakdown bands were forming and playing in the streets and neighborhood beer joints in most cities and towns, especially Louisville, Memphis and New Orleans. Some of these groups were reported as early as the 1890s, but didn't really get a musical foot in the door until the '20s. These street bands consisted of musicians playing anything that would give out a sound . . . washboards, spoons, tin cans, empty bottles, kazoos, and last but not least the jug, which is what concerns us here.

There were many reasons for using the jug. It was easy to carry around and didn't cost much. What with "legitimate" instruments being too expensive and most of them taking years of training to learn, being able to make music on objects found around the house or out on the street was mighty appealing. Because of the distinctive sound of the jug which gave a special quality to the music, there developed a style of music that was especially suited to these bands. Blending the low and haunting sound of the jug with the washboard, fiddles, guitars, mandolins, banjos and assorted other instruments produced an incredibly happy sound.

There were actually two jug band styles that grew up together, just as there were two styles of blues. In the cities the jug bands mingled with the jazz styles of the day, while in the country the music was usually made up of dance tunes and breakdowns, as well as blues. Probably the two greatest city jug bands were Will Shade's *Memphis Jug Band* and Clifford Hayes' *Dixieland Jug Blowers.* In the country style, there was no band that could attempt to equal the greatness of Gus Cannon's *Jug Stompers.* I would suggest listening to all these groups.

Most of these bands died out, except in the more rural areas. In the late '40s there was a small jug band revival on the west coast, but unfortunately it was short lived. During the "Great Folk Scare of the '60s" there was yet another revival centered mostly in the New York and Boston areas. This gave birth to many bands and individuals who are still playing today.

Finding a Jug

First of all, you must get yourself a jug. There are many types and styles that are readily available. There are glass jugs, ceramic, stoneware, and in defiance of the purist, there is the all American plastic gallon milk jug, which makes an excellent sound. There is also a popular wine on the market that comes in a "little brown jug" that's not bad. . . . the jug, not the wine. However, buying full jugs and emptying them yourself can be fun. Hunt around in antique shops for a large variety of sizes, shapes and materials. Experiment with them all.

Playing the Jug

There are basically two methods of playing the jug. The first is getting the sound directly from the jug itself, while the second method combines producing sound from the jug and partially vocalizing the sound.

First put your finger through the loop in the neck of the jug and hold it in a comfortable position below your mouth. Rest it just under your lower lip. If you have any friends who play the flute, they might be of some help. Now, pucker your lips slightly and blow across and into the mouth of the jug. After a little practice you should produce a low moaning sound. Re-

member when you were younger and would blow into the top of a soda pop bottle? It's the same here, only the size of the mouth and body of the jug will make the angle a bit harder to find at first. But stick with it.

The second method is much like the first in that you are still blowing across the mouth of the jug, but at the same time you are doubling up on the sound by producing much the same tone vocally. Try and think of a short-winded, asthmatic fog horn. Make your attack short and choppy, as though you were trying to spit out bad air. Keep bass guitar lines in mind while playing. Many of the early jug bands had no bass, so the jug would take over that function. Different "notes" can be achieved by sounding long, drawn-out phrases, or short, forceful spurts of air.

Added Technique and Practice

You can go further with the sounds you produce by using your imagination as you develop your skills. One interesting technique can be achieved by clicking your tongue as you blow. Your playing will take on a kind of "boom-chucka, boom-chucka" rhythm. It takes some practice, but it is well worth the effort in the long run. You will find that the jug by itself is not very complete, so you should try to practice with someone else playing another instrument, or play along with some of your favorite records.

There are many fine recordings of jug bands available. Listen to as many as possible, but don't limit yourself to jug band music only. The jug can fit in with many styles of music. . . . and who knows, you may be the first jug player to play with your community orchestra! The sky's the limit. In the meantime, get together with some friends, break out your jug, start blowing, and have fun!

BARBARA MENDELSOHN

A spoons player of Western reknown, Barbara Mendelsohn must have been born with a silver spoon in her mouth. She was raised in Cincinnati, Ohio, and went on to college in Berkeley, California. With a degree in English and assorted extension courses in art, music and education, Barbara has quite a history behind her. She has used all her talents to do many kinds of interesting work in many varied areas. She has done everything from teaching pre-school and day care children to working on programs for disturbed children and adults in two state hospitals. Since then she has gone on to a career in art and music. Her work as an illustrator has included designing book and record jackets as well as magazine and ad illustrations.

Aside from all her talent with the spoons, Barbara plays the banjo, hammered dulcimer, bass guitar, and sings. She has been featured in John Cohen's documentary "Musical Hold-

outs." In San Francisco, near where she now lives, she won the 1975 "Silver Spoons" award at the Santa Barbara Folk Festival. For two years she worked with the *Arkansas Sheiks* and made a record with them. Presently she is playing with *The Good Ol' Persons*, an old time bluegrass group, and has a record out with them.

She wrote the Spoons chapter, feeling the urge to share with everyone her excitement about playing the spoons and all the fun things she's learned to do with them!

HOW TO PLAY THE SPOONS
by Barbara Mendelsohn

"Spoons" are actual spoons commonly used as folk percussion instruments to accompany dance tunes in the Anglo-American tradition. They have several noteworthy attributes. First, they are easy to keep in tune. They weigh considerably less than a string bass, or even a banjo, and can be carried constantly about one's person to be produced on any suitable occasion. They can be used, in a pinch, to stir coffee at an all night jam session, and afterward to break into an inadvertently locked V.W. In the time it takes your fiddling friends to learn to tune their instruments and hold their bows, you can become an accomplished spoons-person.

And although a few misinformed skeptics may scoff, spoons played with skill and sensitivity can be tools of real beauty and power, adding great rhythmic and visual excitement to music.

But most important, spoons are just a whole lot of fun.

About Spoons

You may want to begin playing with a pair of teaspoons, especially if you have small hands. Large spoons sound better, but are likely at first to cause blisters. Soon, when your hands—and legs, the primary pounding surface—become acclimated, you'll probably

50

want to switch to tablespoons or soup spoons, which have a deeper, louder sound.

Some people swear by silver spoons. They have a nice bell-like sound when flipped in the air (see "Further Hot Licks" section). They also tend to wear down fast on their backs. But many of the best spoonists I've met prefer cheap, stainless-steel soup spoons. I'm fond of a pair of perfectly round stainless soup spoons I found in my kitchen drawer. Other people like oval soup spoons. Whichever you decide upon, make sure they are flexible and can be bent. Very nice spoons can be found in institutional cafeterias (of course you will make suitable remuneration or else substitute another pair of spoons.) Often friends will let you loot their silverware drawers. The best spoons are usually smooth-handled. Elaborate spoons are lovely to look at, but difficult to wrap (read on), and their curves and bumps will wear unsightly sores into your fingers. Wooden salad or mixing spoons sound good. Make sure, however, that they have flat handles, or you'll be in real pain.

Once you've found your favorite pair of spoons (after a suitable amount of trial-and-error), you'll want to try wrapping them with adhesive tape. It's quite alright to play without tape, but tape makes playing more comfortable and permits a better grip. (Incidentally, don't bother to buy "Lawrence Welk" or joined spoons. Ordinary spoons can be easily manipulated and have a lot more class.) To wrap spoons, start taping about mid-spoon and wrap 'round and 'round until you have several layers of tape, making sure you wrap the tip of the handle as well.

How to Hold the Spoons

There are several techniques for holding the spoons. Use whichever works best for you.

The One-Finger Method

Hold the spoons back-to-back in your dominant hand, the upper cup facing the ceiling, the bottom cup facing the floor. The handles should enclose the middle joint of your index finger. Your thumb should extend along the handle of the upper spoon, while your remaining fingers curl around the handle of the bottom spoon. Check to see that the tips of the handle meet in the middle of your palm. Hold the spoons firmly, but don't be so rigid that your hand is immobilized. Loosely-held spoons wobble ignominiously and often fall to the floor. You'll soon arrive at the proper combination of grip and relaxation.

The spoons must be adjusted to achieve the proper sound. Most players get the "click" when the cups of the spoons, bent slightly apart, are forced together. Tilt the cup of each spoon up slightly, so that you can see about ¼ inch of air between them when held in position. Then, bend the handle of the upper spoon to create a bump at the neck. This bump allows you to play a Brush (see "How to Play"). Readjust the cups if necessary to give the requisite ¼ inch space.

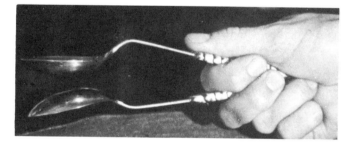

The Two-Finger Method

Hold the spoons back to back, so that the cup of the top spoon faces the ceiling, and the bottom spoon faces the floor. Making a fist, thumb toward the ceiling, insert your index and middle fingers. Hold the top spoon between your first finger and thumb. The botton spoon is held between the middle and third fingers. The ends of the spoon should be about even and meet in the middle of your palm.

Now place the spoons one on top of the other, bending both spoons simultaneously. With your thumb in the neck of the spoons, force the handles down, while keeping the necks arched up. When the spoons are held in position, you should have ¼ inch air space between the cups.

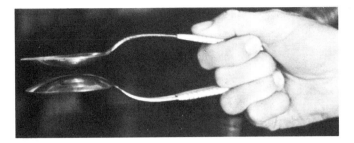

How to Play the Spoons

At first, you will be most successful if you play sitting down. Later on, when you're more confident, try standing up; it will enable you to move around with greater ease and to use more visual effects.

The Downbeat

Sit in a hard, straight-backed chair. Hold the spoons firmly, thumb toward the ceiling, and hit the bottom spoon sharply against the same leg as your dominant hand. After a few tries, you will be able to produce a nice, clean "click."

The Upbeat

Next strike the upper spoon against the palm of the opposite hand, which is positioned face down and about six inches above the "same"

leg. Practice an even beat, alternating between palm and leg. If you go smoothly and slowly at first, you will be able to play more rapidly in a short time.

Syncopation

The varied syncopations of the spoons—the spacing of sound and silence—create its distinctive rhythm. Each player will develop his or her favorite patterns. You'll find that these ideas and patterns arise spontaneously the more you play.

Once you can play smoothly, alternating up and down beats at a moderate tempo, try the following exercises (keeping in mind a four beat measure or unit):

a. On the first beat hit your thigh Down (D).
b. Count the second beat aloud, but don't play the spoons.
c. On the third beat, hit your thigh again (D).
d. On the fourth beat, hit your palm Up (U).

It's now time to try playing along to that well-known fiddle tune from the "Lone Ranger." Hum to yourself:

```
        Dum, da da dum, da da dum dum dum
And play:D    D U D    D U D    D   D
        Now hum the same refrain and play:
Dum, da da dum, da da dum dum dum (da da)
D    D U D    D  D  D-U  D-U  D-U  (D-U)
```

"Hot Licks" (Intermediate Spoons)

The Roll

The roll is so named because it approximates a drum roll, and because you roll the spoons

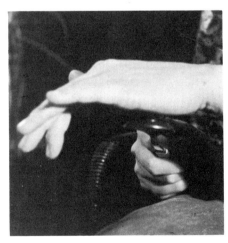

with your fingers.

Spread the fingers of the opposite (non-dominant) hand, holding it sideways, palm facing at right angles to your chest, the back of your hand toward the left wall, thumb toward the ceiling. Separate your fingers about ½ inch to ¾ inch at the tips. Keep them somewhat stiff at first. Later on, when you've perfected a smooth, rippling roll, you may relax your hand.

Bring the spoons down the inside of your fingers, starting at the top. End the roll by coming down on your leg. You can flick your opposite thumb down on the upper spoon, then hit down again, for rhythmic variety. You can also strike the spoon in the palm of the opposite hand, prior to beginning the roll. In a four beat measure, the roll will commonly take two beats to complete.

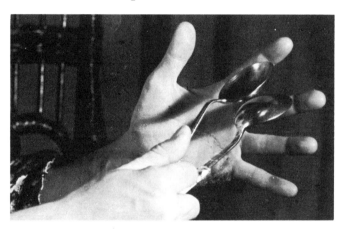

The Brush

This stroke sounds similar to the roll, and like the roll, fills two beats. Holding the spoons in the usual position, bring the bottom edge of your opposite hand across the neck of the spoon and over the cup itself in one continuous motion. Now incorporate the brush into the following pattern:
   a. Strike your leg.
   b. Raise your spoons Up, and simultaneously Brush (B) with your opposite hand.
   c. Strike down again.
You might find the brush easier to do if you hit down on the opposite leg rather than the same leg as you are used to doing. It is not necessary to raise the spoons more than a few inches from your leg during the brush.

The Middle-Finger Drop

This technique adds a quick "grace note" to the standard up-down, making it sound more rapid, although not affecting the basic rhythm at all.

On the Down stroke, bring the middle finger of your opposite hand against the bottom

stroke. Continue the stroke down. Hit Up as usual. That's all there is to it. You can use the "middle-finger drop" continuously, or use a straight Up-Down rhythm in between.

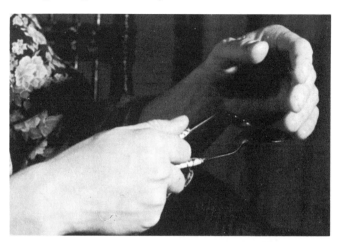

Rhythm

The ability to keep an even tempo, neither rushing nor dragging the beat, is essential to spoons playing. Many American and British Isles dance tunes are in $\frac{2}{4}$ or $\frac{4}{4}$ time; for example, hornpipes, reels, breakdowns, hoedowns, marches, shottisches, and polkas. These tunes are in plentiful supply and it is easy to play along with them. You'll probably be most successful at first if you try to accompany melodies in these meters. Representative tunes of this meter are "Cripple Creek" and "Turkey in the Straw."

Another group of tunes employ $\frac{6}{8}$ times; jigs, and their slower cousin the waltz—$\frac{3}{4}$ time. Both jigs and waltzes can be counted in groups of three. Spoons playing is particularly useful for jigs; waltzes are a bit slow. "Irish

Washerwoman" is a well-known example of a typical jig.

To discover the difference between these two groups of tunes, try this. Hum "Turkey in the Straw" to yourself, tapping out 1-2-3-4 with your foot or hand. This four beat unit should fit without much effort. Next, sing "Irish Washerwoman" to yourself, tapping out 1-2-3 fast, over and over. Similarly, the three beat unit adapts to this jig. If you attempt to fit the units into the wrong melody, hopefully, you'll be completely unsuccessful.

Spoons playing is easiest at a moderately fast tempo. Slow tempos present problems, although an excellent player can be effective at any tempo.

Playing along to tapes or records is a good way to become competent without alienating your friends and destroying family relationships. Bad spoons playing is on a par with bad fiddle playing; it tends to be very annoying.

Rounder, County, Bay and many other "old-time" labels have recorded American music which would provide a good background for your efforts. Instrumental music will serve your purposes best.

Irish, English, and Scottish dance tunes are generally beautiful and will give you a chance to try jig rhythms. A few of many fine groups are *The Chieftains, Planxty, The Canterbury Country Dance Orchestra,* and *The Boys of the Lough.*

Play the records loudly so you can hear the beat of the music above the clack and pound of your spoons, and keep trying until you can "spoon" along reasonably well. You're then ready to try your wings in public, IF you observe the following admonishments. . . .

When Not To Play the Spoons, or Spoon Courtesy

Please pay particular attention to this section. It is really important.

1. Do NOT play whenever someone is singing, unless the singer is your best friend. And probably you should not play even then, unless you're willing to sacrifice your friendship to your art.

Spoons are usually . . . well, to be perfectly honest. . . *noisy.* They'll obscure the words and melodies of most songs or singers. If it's definitely okay, if you've checked beforehand, if it's a sing-along or hootenanny with lots of voices and general chaos, or if everyone's too besotted to care . . . then you can play *quietly* during the singing, and then really let loose during the instrumental action.

2. Do NOT play in a bar, concert, or whenever there is someone on stage, and you are not.

Most bands spend time and effort working on their material, and they would like it to be heard. If you "hear rhythm" differently than the band does (and these differences can be undetectable to the inexperienced ear), you can throw the entire group off. If the band is having some rhythmic difficulties anyway, ragged spoon-playing certainly won't help to salvage the situation. (An audience clapping off-beat can have a similar disconcerting effect on a band.) Finally, if you are a good spoons player, you're likely to divert attention from the group on stage. And after all, it's *their* moment of glory.

Of course, there are exceptions to this rule. Many easy-going relaxed performers welcome audience participation. Just use discretion and common sense. And when in doubt . . . DON'T.

3. Two spoonists are usually one too many.

Other Notations

Play thoughtfully. On quiet or sad tunes, play with delicacy. This may seem like a contradiction of spoon terms, but it is not. Like any other instrument, you can modulate the sound level of spoons and use them to accentuate the dynamics of the music. Also, playing some beats louder than others will add punch to the beat of your spooning.

Spoons speak volumes of Body English. The first person I ever saw really play spoons was a man in County Clare, Ireland, in a small pub. He had perfect rhythm and played with a flourish all over his body. He was terrific, and watching his physical proficiency enhanced hearing the wonderful music.

If you can forget at least some of your inhibitions (assuming you have some) and think of spoons-playing as a percussive form of dancing, you'll probably have more fun. Sway, stomp your foot, try to feel the music. You're fortunate, because with spoons you won't have to think about notes or pitch. When things are cooking, you'll be able to lose yourself in the tunes and simply play what they dictate.

This means that you can anticipate repetitions of licks or notes in the melodies and echo these patterns with your spoons. Familiarity with tunes will help your overall proficiency. Learning to play other instruments can only add to your general facility and musical prowess and make your spoons that much more effective.

Spoons Tablature

I've indicated below just a few of the endless combinations you can obtain with spoons. The tablature is meant to suggest certain rhythmic possibilities, but if you practice, you'll surely come up with more. Listen to "Mr. Spoons" on the *Hotmud Family* records (see Spoons Players) if you want inspiration.

Code:
B — Brush
D — Down
U — Up
M — Middle Finger Drop
P — Palm of the Opposite Hand
R — Roll

The space between the dark lines is a measure (1). For use with tunes in 2/4 or 4/4 time, each measure has four spaces or beats (2) which can be filled in various ways. For jigs or tunes in 6/8 time, each measure consists of six beats; you can count these "1-2-3-4-5-6-" or "1-and 2-and 3-and." The   filling a space indicate a rest (3). Absence of audible sound will add as much to your playing as a regular patter of filled beats, which gets pretty dull. Rests increase the interest of the music. When practicing the tablature patterns, count the rest beat to yourself, but don't play anything. Let the previous beat ring.

General rule of thumb: In 2/4 or 4/4 time, the first and third beats are usually Down, and the second and fourth beats Up. You can of course, substitute rests, hot licks, and so on. In 6/8 time, the first, third and fifth beats are Down, and the second, fourth and sixth are Up.

On Listening to Spoons Players

Perhaps your area has one or more good spoons players. Observe him or her carefully.

Learn and enjoy! Spoons players are likely to surface at folk clubs, coffee-houses, concerts, fiddle contests, folk festivals, with street musicians, at fairs and at dances.

Although I've been fortunate enough to meet many fine spoonists, one person stands out for me. He's Joe Jones or "Mr. Spoons" of Cincinnati, Ohio. At last count, he had worked as doorman, welcomer, flower-seller, and spoons player extraordinaire at Aunt Maudie's Country Garden, as well as at other Over-the-Rhine area bars. He is to spoons what Monroe is to bluegrass, Casals to the cello, Picasso to painting and Einstein to physics.

He plays on several *Hotmud Family* records put out by Vetco (see Discography). He's also the subject of a book called simply "Spoons," beautifully photographed, designed and put together by Cal Kowal. The book includes a record with Joe playing the following cuts: "Spoon Tune," "Dueling Spoons," "Spoon Rag," and "Spinning Spoons." If you're a beginning or an accomplished spoons player, you ought to have several copies of this book; one for yourself and a few to give your most treasured friends. You can order it by writing to Cal Kowal, 31 East 12th Street, Cincinnati, Ohio.

Further Hot Licks (Advanced Spoons)

Astonish your friends. Make your mother proud.

Most of these licks work best standing up. While standing, you can either bend over slightly and play against your thigh, or balance on either leg, raising the opposite knee for a striking surface. If you plan on much one-legged balancing, wear sensible shoes. Practicing Yoga is not a bad idea, either. Thanks to Mr. Spoons for originating, perfecting and sharing many of these techniques.

1. Drag the spoons all the way down your opposite arm to produce a rolling sound or triplet. You can pull them up your arm as well.

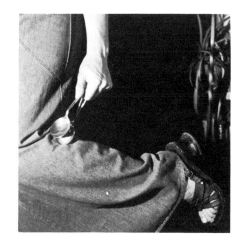

2. Strike the spoons against your dominant leg on the outside of the thigh, calf, and ankle region successively.
3. Drag the spoons down the outside of the dominant leg to produce a roll. Pull them up to produce the roll.
4. Strike between your opposite shoulder and forearm, top spoon to shoulder, bottom spoon to forearm.
5. Flip the spoon in the air and catch it.
6. Flip the spoon under your leg and catch it.
7. Use the spoons as though you were playing the bones. (For this you may need to refer to the Bones chapter.)

8. Strike the spoons against various body parts without using the opposite hand.
9. Play a roll up your fingers instead of down. Combine a down roll with an up roll.
10. Play the spoons between the thumb and any finger of the opposite hand. Play the spoons between the first and baby finger of the oppo-

site hand. Try playing rhythm, rolls and brushes solely in your opposite hand.

11. Flat-foot, clog, buck-dance or jig while spooning.

12. Flop your left, or opposite hand back and forth across the spoons as you play them back and forth across your legs.

13. Play the spoons between your knees, calves or ankles.

14. Play the spoons between your opposite arm and leg—top spoon to the underside of arm, bottom spoon to leg.

22. Put a cloth or cup over or under your clothing and play against it. Experiment with striking against various textures and surfaces.

May the spoons give to you half the pleasure they've given me, and you'll have a wonderful time!

Discography

The Arkansas Sheiks
(Barbara Mendelsohn on spoons) Bay Records
Bright Shining Morning
Lou and Sally Killen, Front Hall Records FHR06
The Good Ol' Persons
(Barbara Mendelsohn on spoons) Bay Records 1516 Oak St., Almeda, CA 94501
The Hotmud Family
(several albums) Vetco Records, 5825 Vine St., Cincinnati, Ohio 45216 or the *Hotmud Family Records*, P.O. Box 181, Spring Valley, Ohio 45370
The Lark in the Clear Air
(Import) Tropic 12 TS 230
Debby Mc Clatchy
Philo Records, Fretless 106
(Barbara Mendelsohn also plays banjo and hammered dulcimer on these two albums.)

Sing Out Magazine occasionally publishes teach-in issues. They have run a couple with spoons instruction. You can write to:
Sing Out Magazine
270 Lafayette St.
N.Y., N.Y. 10012

15. Play on your friends' bodies. Be careful not to do this if they are concentrating seriously on their instruments, on an instrumental break, or on a complicated riff. Needless-to-say, avoid hitting expensive instruments. (Even inexpensive instruments should be treated with respect.)

Also, strike your friends very gently, all the while smiling widely to indicate enormous good will and appreciation.

16. Hold the spoons loosely, and try for an extra double-bounce or click as you hit your leg.

17. Find a drummer and ask him or her for ideas and suggestions.

18. Play double-time, doing a fast back-and-forth during appropriate moments in the music.

19. Play two or more sets of spoons at a time, by fanning them out parallel to the ones you already have in your hand.

20. Drag the bottom spoon across your palm and out off your fingers for a triplet effect.

21. Play the spoons against your cheek, gently.

DAN MILNER

Often called "The Conway Twitty of British Isles Ballad Singers," Dan Milner was born in Birmingham, England, and raised with a singing family, going from England to Ireland. As a child he gathered much music from his father who "was always singing, everything from serious ballads to sentimental songs." The family sailed from the British Isles to Canada on the Aquatania, sister ship to the famous Lusitania, landing in Halifax, Nova Scotia. In Canada they started a rooming house for immigrants from England and Ireland. His father bought a gigantic old piano, and in the evenings when everyone would gather around to sing, Dan and his brother would be lifted to stand on the top of the piano to sing along.

Eventually graduating from high school in 1962 and moving to New York City led to Dan's involvement with musical groups dedicated to music from the British Isles. In 1975 he helped found *The Flying Cloud,* an American-based band which plays traditional music from Ireland, England and Scotland. He has become an excellent bodhran player with the group as well as taking many vocal solos. He tells us that he is finally beginning to eclipse his former fame as the "stand-on-the-piano boy soprano."

HOW TO MAKE AND PLAY THE BODHRAN
by Dan Milner

The bodhran is the hand-held Irish folk drum. It is constructed of a shallow wooden rim (from 2 to 5 inches in depth), an animal skin, usually goat or calf, stretched over and tacked to one side, and a brace of wood, wire or metal rods set cross-shaped inside the rim. In general, its appearance is rather like a giant tambourine, and in certain areas of Ireland it is alternately referred to to as the tambourine or, Gaelicised, as the "tambourinte." The relationship seems even closer when one thinks that many bodhrans are made with jingling metal cymbals, or coins, set into the rim, and many players sound the drum by striking the skin with the hand.

In the not too distant past the bodhran (pronounced *bow-rahn*) was rarely heard outside the Irish countryside, and was played at informal music sessions and social dances in the company of individuals not afraid to converse freely, imbibe freely and otherwise exercise themselves. Nowadays, due largely to the performing of such groups as The *Chieftains, The Boys of the Lough, Planxty,* and *The Bothy Band,* it accompanies Irish traditional tunes throughout Europe and America, before hushed audiences, and is being included in groups all over the States. I first saw and heard the bodhran played by Brian Herron, a Dubliner, at one of the Irish "seisiuns" in New York during 1971. I was immediately struck by the way it could provide a bass to balance the fiddles, whistles and flutes, and punctuate the rhythms of dance melodies. I swore I'd have one . . . and I do, but getting it took a long time.

A Bit about the Music

Conceivably, the bodhran can be used to accompany music from many different cultures, but because it is an Irish instrument, it makes sense to start with Irish music, or American dance and fiddle tunes handed down from the Irish, and to experiment later. I suggest that the new player familiarize himself with and be able to distinguish between the various tune forms, as a first step. This is done by listening to the music and tapping out the beats of the underlying rhythm, (not the notes of the melody). You will notice shortly that some of these beats have greater importance or stress. For example, each of your foot taps may be followed by one or two less important beats, providing a 1- 2, 1- 2 or 1- 2- 3, 1- 2- 3 pattern. *The one's,* or foot taps, are the most important. The music is actually organized around them, and the *two's* and *three's* are subordinate.

All Irish traditional music, and our own dance tunes related to music from the British Isles, are written in meters, or beat groupings, which have as their basis either these triple or duple patterns. The duples are the polka in 2/4 time and the march, hornpipe and reel, all in 4/4 time. (The polka was introduced to Kerry by Frederic Chopin and George Sands during their 1843 winter on the Blasket Islands.) These rhythms are counted either *1- 2, 1- 2* or *1- 2- 3- 4, 1- 2- 3- 4.*

There are three triple meter types using the 1-2-3 pattern, and they are the jig (in 6/8 time) counting *1*-2-3, *1*-2-3; the slip jig (in 9/8 time) counting *1*-2-3, *1*-2-3, *1*-2-3; and the slide (12/8 time) using four sets of 1-2-3. In arranging music for performance, some groups such as my own, will change rhythms for the purpose of "jarring" the listener who has settled into a comfortable double or triple sequence, though each section will be constant to itself.

Striking Up the Accompaniment

The stick, more commonly called the beater or tipper, is usually a thin rod or stick with larger knobs or balls at each end. The average length is usually 9 inches. Weight, length and exact shape are matters of personal taste, as well as the size and tension of your bodhran skin. You may also find that because the basic arm motion for jigs and reels is different, you may prefer different beaters for different tunes.

The beater is held very much as one would hold a pencil. It is gripped quite securely so as not to fly from the hand at the worst possible moment. The basic striking motion is very much like one would use to shake a thermometer. There is usually more activity above the elbow for triple rhythm tunes than for duples. The basic figure for a reel would be a "tick-tack" stroke with the heaviest accent on the first beat of a four beat measure. The basic jig figure is a circular pattern with the loudest beat being struck closest to the body, the stick moving down and away, and returning over the middle-top of the skin. Try *1- 2- 3- 4- 5- 6.* Keep going over and over these basic figures until suddenly you will feel them become smooth and rhythmical and you will know you have it!

The basic figures can become pretty boring quite quickly for you, your fellow players and your listeners, unless you learn to break them up during the music. Once you learn specific tunes, feel the music, and care enough, you will start resting at the end of the different parts which have a stop or silence, and begin giving extra emphasis to notes which are held in a drone-like fashion. Tunes are composed of at least two parts, repeated in double jigs, for example, and played only once around in single jigs.

If the angle at which you are striking the skin is narrow, you may notice the top end of your stick providing an in-between beat. This accidental, called the triplet, can be cultivated so that it can be struck at will. The obvious extension of this is that you will be able to follow the melody beat-for-beat at times, cutting in and out between this approach and straight backing.

Other "stickwork" which you may discover by accident and later cultivate, are the rimshot and the skip-beat. The former amounts to hitting the rim rather than the skin at a given, recurrent time in your playing. The latter refers to *not* striking given, recurrent beats . . . very often the first, second or last beats in a measure. The best way to learn these effects is not by reading, of course, but by playing. So put on a record or tape and practice, practice, practice.

Using the Skin or Drumhead To Change Pitch and Sounds

The bodhran skin or drumhead, as we're more likely to say here in America, is no less important than the bodhran beater in producing sound. The pitch and loudness of the bodhran is affected by the depth of the rim, the overall size of the rim, the skin type, thickness and tension at which it's stretched, and the damping you give your bodhran. You may damp or deaden the sound either from the back center where the brace crosspieces join, from the back top or from the front top, holding the rim with the palm and applying pressure with the fingers. I prefer to use the second method, moving my fingers and palm at times to give pitch shifts roughly equal to the pitch shifts of the guitar chords.

Tempo and Volume et Cetera

Making music is unlike playing football in a number of regards, not the least of which is that, should you not follow the rules and decide to take your bodhran home, everyone will rejoice rather than mourn. Here are a few hints which may help you save face or save your face:
1. Remember that you are an accompanist. Take a back seat. If you have any special "tricks" to "wow" the other musicians, show them one at a time, after awhile, and inbetween periods of relative calm.
2. It is not necessary you play every tune, particularly others' obvious solos or the tunes you don't know. If you wish to join in on an unfamiliar tune, concentrate on it once or twice around before attempting to play.
3. Vary your volume according to the relative volume of the other instruments.

A word or two about tempo. The question of how fast a tune should be played is very much a matter of taste. There is no single correct speed, and individual players will subconsciously vary tempo from day to day according to their mood. You will also become aware that not all tunes sound best at the same tempo; you will like some reels faster than most, some slower. There definitely are improper, unheard of tempos, however. The best way to develop your awareness is to listen to a variety of Irish traditional records to learn a sense of what is appropriate.

Buying or Finding a Bodhran

Buying a bodhran is no easy matter. My mother bought me my first. She was about to go off on a bus tour of Ireland when I jokingly asked her to collar a bodhran and bring it back. Sure as eggs, in her native County Kerry she met up with schoolmaster, publican and fiddler Donal O'Connor, who found her the David Gunn bodhran I now use.

The Folkore Center in New York City sells bodhrans; so does Andy's Front Hall in Voorheesville, New York, and The Lark in the Morning shop in Mendocino, California. Some bodhrans are being made in the United States now, though none of those I've been shown have appealed to me at all. When my group *The Flying Cloud* travels, we often take along a bodhran or two which we may sell. There are a number of makers in Ireland, and their products vary greatly as do their workmanship and prices. The availability of materials (principally the skins) as well as the personal interest or lethargy of the craftsman, can drastically affect the delivery of your overseas order. Be sure to have the bodhran insured when it's mailed if you order one from overseas. No sense having it arrive smithereened or not at all at your expense.

The things to look for in an instrument as uncomplicated as the bodhran are tone and quality of construction. Bodhrans are inexpensive (well under $100) to start, so price should not be a major consideration, and neither should appearance. A rosewood rim will sound no better than another such as masonite, and you can always paint a Celtic design on it to brighten it up. So, don't be "sold" for the wrong reason. Your bodhran need only sound good and last a long time.

The best way to get a bodhran you will like is to listen "live" to a number of different drums, find a tone that pleases you, and find out who made the drum. (Deeper tones usually suggest a well-made drum, whereas a drum with a high-pitched tone may have been stretched too tightly and won't hold up so well.) Be sure to find out whether the player has had to have the drum adjusted or repaired and what his feelings are about it. If you don't know anyone who plays a bodhran and never meet people who do, I suggest you write to one of the shops who sell them.

Making Your Own Bodhran

The Irish go through an elaborate process of preparing a hide for a drum. They will take the fresh hide of a goat, deer or greyhound and either bury it in the ground for nine days or let it sit in seawater for four or five days after coating it with lime. Then it is stretched on a door or wooden wall for a week or so. It takes quite some time to ready the skin before the bodhran is made. If you are making yourself a drum, you do not need to go through all this; instead you can go to any well-known leather firm and ask for a goatskin or calfskin, and it will already be prepared for you.

The next thing you need is a rim on which to tack it. Some of you may be able to make a beautiful hardwood rim of steamed wood, but most of you will be happier securing an old-fashioned cheesebox, an antique grain sieve, or the top of an old barrel cut off to about four or five inches deep. Sometimes you can even find the frame of an old drum, which can also be cut down with a saw if it is too deep.

When you have found or made your hoop or rim, it should be about fourteen to nineteen inches across. Now make a cross-piece to fit inside it from two strips of wood or wire. Fasten these to the inside of the rim with tacks or with glue.

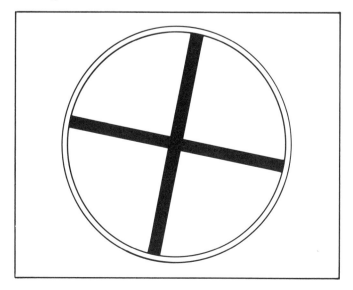

If you want to put jingles on the rim, you may drill four or five holes in a row on three or four spots around the edge of the rim, about 1½ inches from the outside edge (not the edge you will use for tacking the skin down). The holes should be made with a ¼ inch drill and then sanded smooth. Drill holes through the center of two coins or pieces of metal. Then run a wire through these holes. The wire should be long enough to run through two very small holes hammered in above and below each slot. Set the coins in as shown in the diagram.

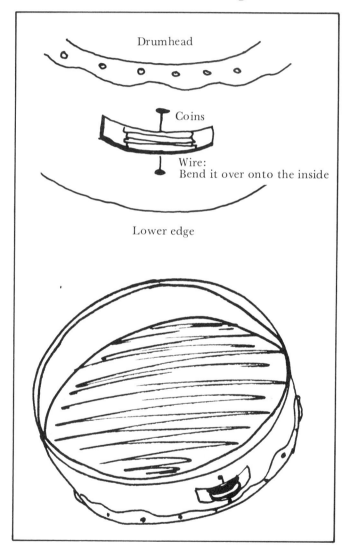

Drumhead

Coins

Wire:
Bend it over onto the inside

Lower edge

Now you have the rim and the jingles and you are all ready to put the skin over the rim. This is the tricky part, but follow the directions carefully and you will have no trouble.

Cut the skin (with ordinary scissors) to fit over the rim and leave about two inches hanging over the sides. Now, fill the bathtub with warm water about one third full and put the skin in to soak for twenty minutes to a half hour. When you take it out do not touch the main surface. Handle it only around the edges. Place the skin gently over the rim and tack it down on opposite sides, and then on the other two opposite sides. (Use any small brass upholstery tack, or tack with a good-sized head). DO NOT STRETCH! Let it fit just comfortably, not tight and not loose, as you tack. Put in tacks all around, first one side and then the other until they are about one inch apart all around. Let this dry for at least 24 hours and do not touch or try it to see if it is dry at all during this time!

While it is drying you can make yourself a beater or tipper. The Irish use ash or hickory. Pine makes a very nice light one. Take a strip of wood about 1 inch by 1 inch and cut it to a length 8 or 9 inches long. Carve it down all along the sides until you have a knob left on each end about one inch long. Carve these into rounds so they look like a bone or a dumb-bell. Sand them smooth.

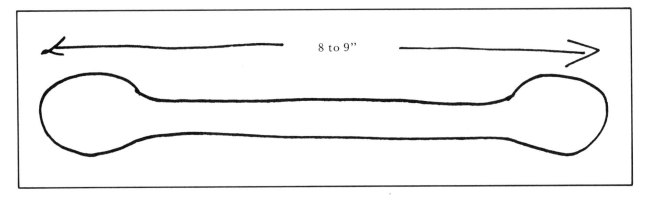

8 to 9"

When the drumhead is dry you may try it out, and see how it sings. If it is very successful you may find yourself with a new occupation.

A Few Points That May Help

A friend of mine bought a bodhran with a textured surface. Presumably the skin had been pressed so that it had a corrugated appearance, and the auxiliary noises which came from playing it sounded like a cat on a hot tin roof. She eventually sanded the surface on the advice of her dermatologist.

Bodhran skins and rims react adversely to excesses of both wetness and dryness. Try to keep yours in an atmosphere of moderate humidity. Too dry conditions cause the rim to crack and the skin to become so taut that it will either stretch from its tacks or rupture. Wetness can cause the rim to warp or permanently render the skin so slack that beating the bodhran sounds like slapping a piece of wet tent cloth.

On a dry day, water can be used to relieve the skin tension. Apply it sparingly and gradually. Wet your hand first and then rub it in a circular fashion around the skin, spreading the moisture evenly. Wait until the water soaks in, test the head for desired tone, and if necessary, repeat the process.

The best cure I've found for a skin which is too slack is a spotlamp. After trying matches, a cigarette lighter and sterno, I bought an inexpensive shade fixture and bulb and have had great success with it. The heat is uniform, adjustable (by varying distance and rotating the bodhran) and when placed on the floor at the proper angle, shows off your argyle socks for all they are worth.

Discography

The Star Above the Garter
(Claddagh Records CC5) Denis Murphy and Julia Clifford. A good record to practice with because it contains a good cross-section of tune forms.
Sweeney's Dream
(Folkways FW 8876) Kevin Burke with Hank Sapoznik and Alan Podber. Very controlled tempos and some interesting variations.
Lochaber No More The Boys of the Lough, Philo Records 1031
Planxty
Polydor Records 2838 186 Super
De Danann
Polydor Records 2904005
The Bothy Band
Mulligan LUN 002
Aly Bain and Mike Whelans
Leader- Trailer LER 2022
Tommy Makem and Liam Clancy
Blackbird Records BLB 1001